KIDNAP AND RANSOM: The Response

by the same author

ACROSS THE RIVER (as Richard Jocelyn)—Constable
THE LONG LONG WAR—Cassell
PROTEST AND THE URBAN GUERRILLA—Cassell
RIOT AND REVOLUTION IN SINGAPORE AND MALAYA
  1945–1963—Faber and Faber
LIVING WITH TERRORISM—Faber and Faber
GUERRILLAS AND TERRORISTS—Faber and Faber
BRITAIN IN AGONY—Faber and Faber

KIDNAP AND RANSOM:
The Response

Richard Clutterbuck

FABER AND FABER
London · Boston

First published in 1978
by Faber and Faber Limited
3 Queen Square London WC1
Printed in Great Britain
by Latimer Trend & Company Ltd Plymouth
All rights reserved

British Library Cataloguing in Publication Data

Clutterbuck, Richard
Kidnap and ransom.
1. Terrorism 2. Kidnapping—Political aspects
3. Ransom—Political aspects
I. Title
364.1'54   HV6431

ISBN 0–571–11306–0
ISBN 0–571–11327–3   Pbk

Contents

Foreword

SIR ROBERT MARK, G.B.E., Q.P.M.

THE author is one of a small but select number who have joined the academic world after a successful career in the armed forces. A Senior Lecturer in Politics at Exeter University since 1972 he retired from the Army in the rank of Major-General on relinquishing the post of Chief Army Instructor at the Royal College of Defence Studies. Understandably, he has maintained a close interest in kidnapping, terrorism, subversion and other violent and unlawful activities with political, as well as criminal, implications. He has earlier written a number of books on this subject, on which he also lectures regularly to the police, the army and industry.

This particular volume is designed as a useful and handy work of reference and guidance, rather than a study in depth, about activity which in recent years has increasingly attracted worldwide attention. In a country like Great Britain in which kidnapping is rare and thought, to say the least, to be unlikely the book has perhaps a special value in that it brings home forcefully the realization just how widespread kidnapping and hostage-taking is throughout the world and, even more disturbing, how it has flourished in social, economic and political conditions favourable to it. Few if any reading it would disagree that it is now necessary to make a special study of kidnapping and similar unlawful activities, notwithstanding our relative freedom from both. Indeed, Roy Jenkins, when Home Secretary, took the initiative in exploring with neighbouring E.E.C. countries the possibility of ministerial and police liaison necessary to counter them on a European basis, a farsighted move indeed. It is known also that some of the largest and most vulnerable international commercial undertakings are taking steps to guard against or to prepare for such a threat. It can therefore be said without question that the book is worthwhile for its crisply factual account of the problem, more than sufficient to persuade the complacent of the need to recognize the threat and to take it seriously.

The author describes briefly the operation of kidnapping and hostage-taking in many countries, details the differing methods, operations and motives of those responsible and the difficulties in countering them. So many case histories in one book inevitably and unconsciously tend to give the impression that this kind of activity enjoys internationally a greater degree of co-ordination than I think the evidence justifies but the author is, I think, right in suggesting that there has been a limited degree of subsidy and support by governments seeking to promote unrest in other states.

The book allows the tentative conclusion that, given similar resources of manpower, organization, equipment and weapons, as between one country and another, the overriding feature determining success or failure in countering kidnapping will almost certainly be the reaction of the government or security forces dealing with each particular incident, their preparedness, experience and perhaps most important their relationship with the society they serve. In a stable and reasonably well-balanced society, terrorism and kidnapping, seen objectively, are never likely to be more than an unpleasant though sometimes tragic nuisance. Indeed, they may be counterproductive by alienating effectively the whole of society. In countries not enjoying reasonable stability, however, kidnapping, hostage-taking and terrorism can have a disproportionately upsetting effect.

Dr Clutterbuck's book is welcome if not overdue because he compels recognition at last of kidnapping or hostage-taking on a scale justifying intensive study, precautions, counter measures and co-ordination both within particular countries and internationally. Read superficially it is rather alarming; considered objectively it is a useful and timely warning of the need to be prepared for, but not daunted by, the unpleasant prospects it unfolds.

ROBERT MARK

Preface

I CONSULTED many people in writing this book, including kidnap victims, their families and colleagues, police, army and other security force officers, prison officers, embassy officials, security consultants, members of security firms, executives and security directors of corporations, journalists and other witnesses. Soon after the kidnappings of Hanns-Martin Schleyer and Aldo Moro I visited Germany and Italy, and I also had discussions with people from Argentina, Belgium, Canada, Chile, the Netherlands, Sweden and the USA.

Most of these people, both in the UK and overseas, prefer for obvious reasons that they should not be quoted by name, and I have therefore quoted none by name, except for a number of public figures whose views in general are already well known, such as Sir Geoffrey Jackson and Sir Robert Mark. I would however, particularly like to acknowledge the help I have received from the staff of Control Risks Ltd., who have extensive practical knowledge of this problem worldwide; and from Peter Hamilton of Chubb Security Services Ltd., who has justly earned the reputation of being one of the leading thinkers in the field of protection against terrorist attack.

I am most grateful to the Wolfson Foundation, who provided a grant to support my research, the major part of which was used to give me a research assistant, Louise Perry. She is an ex-policewoman with a law degree and has contributed enormously, as a friend as well as a professional colleague, to this book.

In writing a book like this, an author always faces the dilemma of whether to include material which might help terrorists as well as their potential victims or the police. I faced the same dilemma in my earlier book, *Living with Terrorism*. In aiming for the right balance I have taken account of the material already available to terrorists in revolutionary manuals, such as the one published by the Monteneros (see Chapter Seventeen); also of the detailed press reports and analyses in journals, with diagrams, whenever there is a major kidnapping such as that of Schleyer or Moro. Hostage taking is the most complex and sophisticated of terrorist operations; and it is naïve to imagine that criminals and political terrorists do not plan their operations very carefully, studying all such relevant material. An example of such detailed planning is described in Chapter Seventeen.

The other side of the balance is that the first essential in defence against kidnapping is that all those who have to deal with it should understand the people who do it, their motivations, aims, organizations and techniques; and the second is to understand how to set about reducing the risk of being a victim, and how to manage the crisis if it occurs. If, for fear of telling criminals and terrorists what they already know, we were to insulate ourselves from the means of acquiring this understanding, the balance would be negative.

So the purpose of this book is to contribute to the understanding of terrorists and their techniques, and of the ways to approach the task of countering them.

Exeter, May 1978   RICHARD CLUTTERBUCK

Introduction

ON 16th September 1974 the two Born brothers, sons of the Chairman and founder of Bunge Born of Argentina, were kidnapped from their car by the Monteneros. Though guarded and escorted, they left home at the same time every day to drop their children at school on the way. After being held hostage for nine months, they were released for a ransom of $60 million.

On 27th February 1976 William Niehous, Vice-President of Owens-Illinois in Venezuela, was kidnapped in Caracas by the Commando Armigiro Gabaldon, believed to be a splinter group of the Bandero Roja. The firm conceded to a demand from the kidnappers to publish a manifesto and a condemnation of the Venezuelan Government in newspapers in Venezuela and in London, Paris and New York. The Venezuelan Government announced that it would nationalize the assets of the Owens-Illinois subsidiary for breach of national law in bringing the government into disrepute and publishing a statement produced by a subversive group. The firm also paid a ransom of $1,250,000; but Niehous was never released, and must now be presumed dead. So the firm stood to lose its corporate assets in Venezuela, its $1,250,000 ransom, and its man.

Criminal gangs in Italy have found that the kidnapping of children is particularly profitable. In July 1975, eighteen-year-old Cristina Mazzotti was kidnapped; a ransom of $2 million was paid, but the kidnappers killed her just the same. Another father stood firm for six weeks when his seventeen-year-old daughter was kidnapped, but paid a ransom of $4 million when they threatened to kidnap his other daughter as well. And in 1977

a $2 million ransom was paid for a five-year-old Italian girl
kidnapped on her way to school in Geneva.

These examples illustrate two things: first the catastrophic and
sometimes open-ended losses which a kidnap can cause; and
secondly the need for a hard-headed and professional approach
both to security and to crisis management.

The aim of this book is to indicate how to set about this approach; it makes no attempt to provide cut-and-dried plans for a
particular situation: every family, every factory, every office, has
a different environment and a different problem. While there can
be no watertight security against terrorism, the risk can certainly
be reduced.

So the purpose is to suggest how to identify and assess the risk;
how to manage and reduce that risk; how to prepare for crisis
management; how to approach negotiation with kidnappers; and
how best to co-operate with the police at every stage, ideally to
help them to detect where the hostage is held so that he can be
rescued or, failing that, to enable the police to arrest and convict
the kidnappers after the victim is released.

Perhaps most important of all, the book may indicate the areas
in which a family or firm will do well to seek professional advice
about their own particular case, and suggest what questions they
should ask: from the police; from their lawyers; from insurance
brokers; from security consultants or firms. It may be necessary
to get an expert assessment of the threat in a particular country
or environment; and to commission a security survey to decide
upon the necessary procedures and physical measures that are
worth taking, and to prepare plans both for prevention and for
reaction.

Kidnapping is not confined to the executives of large firms,
millionaires or their families. Indeed, because the threat has led
to many of these taking better precautions, kidnappers have
turned increasingly to easier targets. The father of 'heiress'
Lesley Whittle (kidnapped and murdered in Britain in 1975) was
a successful self-made man but certainly no millionaire (the
ransom demanded was £50,000—$90,000); farmers in Southern
Italy are frequently required to subscribe to a ransom for the
release of one of the village children; and a substantial number of
'ordinary citizens' have been kidnapped or assassinated because

they were junior executives, politicians, government officials, policemen and soldiers off duty, judges, magistrates, assessors or jurors.

Such an ordinary citizen, who has no reason to believe that he is a particular target, may well be picked as one of several alternative victims to achieve the same end (ransom or political blackmail). His best approach is to take adequate commonsense precautions, at work, at home or on the road, to avoid being a conspicuous and attractive target. The more manifest these precautions are, and the more positive his attitude towards security, the more likely the terrorists are to look around for a 'softer' target.

The origin of the word 'kidnap' is significant: it means 'to seize (nap) a child (kid)'. Like assassination (the implied threat without which kidnapping would lose its power) it has been used ever since human animals first began to combine in hunting groups and tribes. The chief of such a group might be a hard man, giving no quarter and asking none for himself, but could be made to give way when someone seized his child. And kidnapping for ransom, especially of the son and heir, became rife in Europe in the Middle Ages.

The *Encyclopaedia Americana* records the first notorious case of kidnapping for ransom in the USA as that of four-year-old Charley Ross in Pennsylvania in 1874. The kidnappers sent a letter demanding a ransom of $20,000, but were so scared of detection that no one could contact them, and the boy was never ●een again. The rise of gangsterism in the 1920s led to a massive growth of kidnapping for ransom in the USA: in the two years before 1932 there were 200 kidnappings in Chicago alone, and ransoms totalling $2 million were paid.

There was, of course, a strong Italian flavour about the growth of kidnapping and gangsterism in Chicago and New York, because this had for centuries been a common technique for bandits and criminal gangs in Southern Italy, Sardinia and Sicily; it is no surprise that Italy has by far the highest incidence of kidnapping in Europe, and that there are still strong links between the American and Italian Mafia.

The kidnapping and murder of the eighteen-month-old

Lindbergh baby in March 1932 shocked American society into
enacting the death penalty for kidnapping if the victim was harmed or still missing when sentence was passed. There were,
nevertheless, still a great many kidnappings for ransom in the
USA between 1933 and 1935, and a number of the victims were
killed after payment of the ransom to eliminate them as witnesses.

Since 1935 the FBI has achieved a very high conviction rate
for kidnapping. The head of the FBI reported in 1974 that of the
647 cases of kidnapping in the USA since 1934, all but three had
been solved, and over 90 per cent of the kidnappers had been
captured.[1] A major reason for this success has been the FBI's
recognition that the first consideration of all those concerned is
the release of the victim and that their best chance has lain in
using the evidence gained during the process to arrest the kidnappers *after* his release. This attitude has ensured maximum
co-operation from the relatives and colleagues of the victim; and
the figures testify to the wisdom of such an approach.

Rivalling Italy as the Mecca of kidnapping have been certain of
the Latin American countries, with the Iberian influence in place
of the Italian. As in Sardinia, there have always been bandit and
criminal kidnappings in Latin America, but a major change occurred after the failure of rural guerrilla warfare in the subconti-
nent (notably of Ché Guevara in Bolivia) and the switching of
political terrorism to the cities. Since 1968 kidnapping for ransom
in Latin America has been widespread; but, in contrast with
Italy, the motive has generally been political (i.e. to swell the
funds for further operations) rather than personal criminal gain.
The figures have been horrific. In Argentina alone there were
over 400 kidnappings (criminal and political) in 1973.

Elsewhere in the world, it has more often been for political
blackmail: e.g. the release of other terrorists from prison, as by
the Palestinians, the Japanese United Red Army, the German
Red Army Fraction and the South Moluccans in the Netherlands.

Between 1968 and 1974 terrorism became increasingly inter-

1. Cited by Brian Jenkins in *Should Corporations be Prevented from
   Paying Ransoms?* (Rand Corporation, Santa Monica, 1974).

national, with the growth to epidemic proportions of aircraft hijackings, and the kidnapping of diplomats, especially in Latin America. In 1975 the US State Department commissioned the Rand Corporation to prepare a 'Chronology of International Terrorism' for those years.[2] This study included only those acts of terrorism which crossed frontiers or had international repercussions: thus, it excluded criminal kidnappings in Italy but included kidnappings of diplomats in Latin America. Of 507 international incidents, eighty-two were kidnappings, 113 were aircraft hijackings, 200 were bombings and 112 were shooting and other incidents.

These figures are small compared with those for normal crime (there are, for example, some 18,000 criminal homicides per year in the USA alone) but terrorism has far more effect on society. If someone is murdered for money or revenge, few other people feel threatened unless they are connected or acquainted; there is, however, an ancient Chinese proverb which sums up the meaning of the word terrorism: 'Kill one, frighten ten thousand.'

There are, moreover, some disturbing trends. Kidnappings and assassinations are increasing, whereas bombings are declining. This is probably because bombings can be carried out quite easily by unsophisticated groups; selective assassination needs more planning; but kidnapping requires a high degree of organization, including planning, surveillance, intelligence, detailed preparation and the setting up of safe houses. This suggests that the trend is towards more sophisticated groups—and more kidnapping.

Kidnapping for ransom has in recent years proved far more profitable and less likely to lead to conviction than robbing banks —at any rate in some countries, notably in Italy and Latin America. This is another reason for the dramatic growth of kidnapping, and of the size of ransoms, in those countries.

In West Germany, kidnapping has been far more selective, concentrating on public figures, and for political blackmail rather than ransom. In the Netherlands, kidnapping has been very different from elsewhere: the purpose has again been political, but the pattern has been for the kidnapping of large numbers of

2. Brian Jenkins and Janera Johnson, *International Terrorism: A Chronology. 1968–74* (Rand Corporation, Santa Monica, 1975).

people in a known place (on two occasions in trains). The Dutch have had a remarkable record of success in countering these kidnappings.

The handling of this kind of siege situation is obviously very different from, and very much more likely to end successfully than, the handling of a case where a single victim is held in a secret hideout. The art of handling a hidden-hostage situation lies either in locating the hideout and converting it to a siege or raid situation or, as done so successfully in USA, to use discreet detective work *during* negotiation to lead to arrests *after* the victim has been safely released.

Part I of this book looks at the threat: the organization, motives, tactics and techniques of criminal and political terrorists; how they plan and prepare for a kidnapping; how they hold a hostage, negotiate, collect a ransom and hope to avoid being caught; and where their strengths and weaknesses lie.

Part II is the main body of the book; it looks at the response to kidnapping in a pluralist society and the problems of co-operation between parties whose interests may conflict, such as the victim's family, the police and the media; it examines how to reduce the risk of kidnapping; how to prepare for crisis management in case it occurs; the ordeal of the hostage; the techniques of negotiation; and, should payment of a ransom become in-evitable, how it can be kept to a minimum. It examines ways to help the police either to locate the hideout or to catch the kidnappers after the victim is released; and, if the hideout is found, how to conduct a successful siege or raid.

Part III comprises brief case studies to illustrate these things: in England and Ireland, where the police have devised successful techniques for working with the media and for handling sieges; in the Netherlands, where the government has consistently stood firm and the Dutch Marines have carried out some spectacular rescues; in West Germany, where terrorists have now become the most cold-bloodedly professional, but whose GSG 9 squad emulated the Dutch at Mogadishu; in Italy, where criminal kidnapping is big business; and in Latin America, where the political terrorist organizations have been of a size measured in thousands rather than dozens, and where kidnappings are planned like operations of war.

Part IV consists of a brief glance at the prospects for kidnapping in the future.

There can be no definitive answer to kidnapping. This book aims to encourage more people to make kidnapping more difficult; to help people to identify the areas in their own environment at which it is wise to look critically; to recognize what they can do themselves and what they must ask others to do; and, above all, to save more innocent people from losing their liberty or their lives. If it does these things it will have achieved all that such a book can achieve.

I. THE THREAT

Chapter One

Criminal and Political Terrorists

CRIMINAL OR POLITICAL?

KIDNAPPING, hijacking, killing, wounding, robbery, wilful damage, intimidation, extortion and blackmail are all criminal activities, and anyone who practises them can be defined as a criminal. Nevertheless, some definition is needed which differentiates between those groups whose primary aim is the criminal enrichment of the individuals concerned, and those whose primary aim is political change or the extension of their political power. So these will hereafter be described respectively as 'criminal' and 'political' groups.

Their aims, as well as their activities, often overlap. Political terrorists dedicated to liberation and equality are often unable to resist the temptation to embezzle some of the proceeds of ransoms and bank robberies (when Eddie Gallagher was arrested by the Irish police for kidnapping Dr Herrema in 1975, he was already on the IRA's own death list, accused of embezzling £90,000 from bank robberies which he supposedly carried out for the movement). And, on the other side, few Italian or American readers will need reminding of the political power wielded by the Mafia, built upon money as much as upon violence.

CRIMINAL GROUPS

Though the aims of criminal gangs are predominantly financial (through ransoms, extortion or theft), they are not always entirely so. Criminals may also seek revenge, or to intimidate. Blackmail may have other aims as well as making money. Criminal gangs may seek to extract information, either by theft or by coercion;

and here they may venture into partnership with those who operate in the unscrupulous world of industrial espionage, where skills in bugging, theft, intimidation, blackmail—and kidnapping —command a good price.

The organization of criminal gangs ranges across a spectrum almost as wide as that between a multinational corporation and a corner shop. There are major international criminal networks within Europe, and spreading across North and South America. Affiliated members know where they can turn for local currency, forged documents, stolen cars and safe houses—and, in some countries, for introductions to corrupt politicians, officials and policemen.

Going down the scale, every state has its own sophisticated and independent criminal gangs, which may or may not have regular international contacts. They are often directed by 'respectable' men whose overt occupation is in the business world and whose contacts in finance, industry and politics give them the opportunity to gain valuable intelligence and operational guidance, for example on the selection of targets, or on the financial resources of potential kidnap victims. Few of their rank and file, who do the dirty work and operate the logistic and communications infrastructure, know even of their existence, still less of their identity.

Then there are the powerful strong-arm gangs, such as those operating in New York's West Side or London's East End, which may or may not have links with those bigger networks. Their leaders are certainly known to—and feared by—their rank and file, and many others. These gangs are well geared for taking and holding hostages, negotiating and collecting ransoms, and disposing of the money. And, for a price, they can be hired.

At the bottom of the scale is the loner, who may, because of his lack of resources or sheer incompetence, be the most lethal of all, as was shown by the kidnapping and murder of Lesley Whittle in 1975.

POLITICAL GROUPS

The aims of political groups can be divided into the wider and the more immediate ones. Their wider aims may include national or regional independence, minority rights, or world revolution. Their more immediate aims may include publicity, ransom, blackmail and the discrediting, humiliation or demoralization of governments and of their law-enforcement agencies. Publicity can be beyond the dreams of the pre-television age. At the 1972 Munich Olympics, for example, almost all the nations in the world had their cameras and reporters at the games, hooked by satellite to their viewers at home. Eight Palestinian terrorists kidnapped, held and murdered eleven Israeli athletes, enacting a drama which was watched by an estimated 500 million viewers all over the world. While most of those viewers will have been disgusted and repelled, a large number will have become aware of the Palestinian Arab cause, and some at least will have felt some sympathy: 'If someone had occupied my country I would feel like that!' The South Moluccans could similarly argue that the world neither knew nor cared about their cause until they hijacked two trains in Holland in 1975 and 1977. And millions of people followed the ordeal of Hanns-Martin Schleyer in 1977, many perhaps concluding (quite unjustly) that there must be something wrong with German society—which was what the terrorists wanted.

Ransoms, too can be of a size almost beyond comprehension; and the largest on record, such as the $60 million for the Born brothers and the $14 million for the Exxon executive in Argentina in 1974 were both extorted by political movements, the Monteneros and the ERP, not by professional criminals. Most of this money is believed to have been spread under various names over banks in Europe and elsewhere, and has been and will be used to finance more political terrorism.

Political blackmail is no less effective. Five convicted German terrorists were released in exchange for the life of Peter Lorenz in Berlin in 1975, and one of these five is known to have taken two more lives with her own hand at the OPEC kidnapping in Vienna a few months later. The Austrian Government had already shown its readiness to give way when it closed the Schonau transit camp to save the lives of three hostages in 1973. And the Japanese released five terrorists on to the world, with $6 million, to save the passengers of a hijacked plane in September 1977.

The kidnappings by the Japanese Red Army, the German Red

Army Fraction and the Italian Red Brigades are clearly intended, over and above their ransom, blackmail and publicity dividends, to humiliate and discredit the governments of these countries; and, if possible, to provoke them to overreact, thereby forfeiting popular and world support, and increasing sympathy for the terrorists.

CRIMINAL-POLITICAL CO-OPERATION

Political terrorist groups often lack professionalism—though this may grow with experience, as it clearly has in Germany. They may also lack the weapons, safe houses, communications, informer networks and disciplined organization of the established criminal groups. So the criminals have much to offer to the political groups, which sometimes engage criminal gangs on a straight hiring basis. The actual criminals who carry out the crime may be unaware of the identity of the political group, or of its motives, or indeed that there is any political motive at all.

What can the political terrorists offer in return? First, they often have a fast-moving membership of freshly graduated students who try it for a time, quarrel over ideologies, switch to other movements or to fringe journalism, become frightened, bored or hungry, and wander back into the mainstream of society. It is therefore much more difficult for the police to maintain up-to-date records of names and photographs, or to establish durable and reliable intelligence cover, than it is in the criminal gangs. In some of the more authoritarian countries, idealistic student revolutionaries can be engagingly daring in challenging an oppressive system and, provided that they restrain their brutality, they may attract less public hostility than professional criminals. This has applied in a number of Latin American countries—though the reverse is probably the case in Britain and Germany. And political groups will attract a wider clientele of active and passive sympathizers, including some useful lawyers and journalists, than the criminal gangs.

So criminal gangs may sometimes shelter behind political groups, hoping to confuse the police intelligence and to make use of the services of their sympathizers.

Often, however, the terrorists, of whichever kind, will try to conceal any political affiliations, knowing that the government is more likely to intervene if there is a political challenge, and more likely to stand firm against their demands in order to maintain its credibility; it is likely to try to keep out of anything which appears to be a straightforward criminal kidnapping for ransom.

Another confusing factor is that political groups sometimes degenerate gradually into criminal gangs, retaining no more than a façade of a political 'cause', and only the remnant, if any, of allegiance to their political party. This may be because they have become disillusioned, or plain greedy, or because they know they are on the police wanted list and find no option but to make a living as clandestine criminals. By 1975, many of the IRA gangs in Northern Ireland had degenerated to this, with only perfunctory acknowledgement of their brigade HQs and army council. Eddie Gallagher and Marion Coyle were acting in defiance of the IRA when they kidnapped Dr Herrema.

Chapter Two

European Criminals and Terrorists

THE PROVISIONAL IRA

THE Provisional IRA have carried out a relatively small number of kidnappings but a very large number of murders (at least 1,000 since 1971). They are international in only two respects: though based in Ireland, North and South, they operate also in England (which they regard as a foreign country) where they killed about sixty people in the years from 1973 to 1975; and they have received substantial support in the form of arms and money from overseas, both from governments, e.g. the Libyans, and from members of the Irish-American community, which in 1972 provided about $600,000—though by 1977 this had fallen to less than a quarter of that.

Their political headquarters (Provisional Sinn Fein) operates openly and their Army Council clandestinely, both of them in Dublin, where the IRA itself is an illegal organization, as it is in Britain and Northern Ireland. Most of their units operate in Northern Ireland, though there is a large one based just south of the border in Dundalk. These units are referred to in the IRA as 'brigades', 'battalions' and 'companies', but their total hard-core strength probably numbered only about 200 by 1978. These hard-core members operated underground, but were overtly 'unemployed', queuing up to draw the dole each week from British government social security offices. A typical battalion might have six to fifteen of these full-time officers (a commanding officer, adjutant, quartermaster, intelligence officer, etc.) with call on anything up to 100 'volunteers', mainly teenagers, who could be equipped by the quartermaster with guns and grenades, or briefed to plant a shopping-bag bomb in a pub and set the time fuse in operation. Many of these volunteers were unemployed school leavers, also drawing their (very small) dole from British social security offices. The IRA (with their Protestant opposite numbers) are unique amongst world terrorist movements in being recruited almost entirely from the poorest sections of the community, mainly in the Catholic slums of Belfast and Londonderry and in South Armagh (where they can freely cross the border into Dundalk).

In England and in Southern Ireland, similar groups of up to fifteen operate as 'active service units' (ASUs), but in this case without the reserve of casual volunteers to call upon. One of these ASUs, eleven strong and led by Dolours Price, crossed from Ireland to plant four car bombs in London in March 1973; ten of the eleven were arrested as they attempted to board an aircraft for Ireland just before the bombs went off. Another ASU, about nine strong, was recruited by Mick Murray in the Midlands, and this planted the bombs which killed twenty-one people in Birmingham pubs on 21st November 1974. All nine were arrested and convicted.

Another cell was formed in London in 1973 by a man for whom a fictitious death, followed by a funeral, had been staged in Southern Ireland. He came to England and spent the next year building up a cell four or five strong, which in 1974 and 1975 did a series of forty bombings and eight shootings and caused thirteen deaths. Four of this group were arrested in December 1975 after holding two hostages under siege in Balcombe Street. They held out for nearly six days, possibly to give time for other members of the ASU to get out of the country.

THE GERMAN RED ARMY FRACTION

The Rote Armee Fraktion (RAF) in West Germany has twice been broken up by the police, in 1972 and 1975–6, and, though in each case some survived, the present terrorists form a third generation. This is very different in character from the first generation which included Gudrun Ennslin, Andreas Baader and Ulrike Meinhof, and operated from 1968 to 1972. The first generation were idealistic and amateurish. Though they used guns and bombs, they killed few people; and they enjoyed con-

B

siderable sympathy amongst students and older radical intellectuals. The second generation, who operated from 1974 to 1976,
were more professional and more lethal; and, though several
lived on into the next generation, their phase ended with their
failure at Entebbe in 1976.

The third generation of terrorists dates from 1977. They too
are professional and lethal. Their cold-bloodedness has alienated
most of the idealistic student support enjoyed by their predecessors, though there are some older radicals, mainly lawyers, still
helping them. At the end of 1977 there were probably not more
than fifty or sixty still at large, of whom forty-four were known
and on the police wanted list.

The Red Army Fraction is a reflection not of shortcomings in
German society, but of its political stability and economic success. The German system of proportional representation more or
less guarantees a centre-coalition government, which is what the
overwhelming majority of the voters of all parties want. People
with extreme political views have no real hope of controlling or
even influencing any of the three main political parties (in
contrast, for example, to Marxists in the British Labour Party).
Added to this, the steadily rising standard of living in Germany
has resulted in their total rejection by the factory workers. These
things led them to despair of ever changing society, either
through parliament or by agitating the proletariat; so they
turned, in angry frustration, to the bomb and the gun. When
these, too, seemed to be failing, they turned bitterly upon themselves; and six of the first generation have committed suicide in
prison.

The bombing began in 1968 with incendiary attacks on department stores—not only as symbols of capitalism but as the
places where the establishment 'bought' the compliance of the
proletariat with cheap consumer goods. These attacks were led
by Ennslin and Baader. After being arrested, sentenced and
paroled they escaped, but Baader was rearrested. Ulrike Meinhof,
who as a thirty-seven-year-old successful radical journalist had
supported them in print, suddenly took to the gun and staged a
dramatic armed rescue of Baader from custody. For two years
they staged bomb attacks and bank robberies, all surprisingly
amateurish. In 1972 Ennslin, Baader and Meinhof, along with

Jan-Carl Raspe, Holger Meins and several others, were finally arrested and imprisoned.

The group (then usually known as the Baader-Meinhof gang) seemed to have been crushed; but on 9th November 1974 Holger Meins committed suicide in prison, by hunger strike. Two days later the second generation of the RAF (or a group of them under the name of the Second of June Movement) made their first appearance. It was at once clear that they were using a very different technique: selecting public figures as their victims, and killing them in cold blood. On 11th November the President of the Supreme Court, Gunter von Drenkmann, was celebrating his sixty-fourth birthday. Some young men rang the bell, delivering a gift of flowers. Unsuspecting, the judge answered the door, and they shot him dead.

A few weeks later they kidnapped Peter Lorenz, candidate for election as mayor of West Berlin, and the Berlin government gave way to their demands, releasing five of the first generation of convicted terrorists. These eight did not include the best-known 'amateurs' (Ennslin, Baader, Meinhof and Raspe) but did include a number of the younger and more violent members, who were more in line with the new generation, and at least one of them went on to kill two other victims before being recaptured.

Chancellor Schmidt was determined not to allow this humiliation to be repeated, and in April 1975 he encouraged the Swedish Government to stand firm when six RAF terrorists seized the German embassy in Stockholm and held twelve hostages, including the German ambassador. They threatened to shoot the military attaché and, when the Swedish police refused to withdraw from the building, they did shoot him and threw him down the stairs, mortally wounded. For an hour they kept him covered as he bled, and only then allowed two policemen, stripped to their underpants, to carry him away to hospital to die.

The Swedish government, in direct touch with Bonn, still refused to give way; so six hours later the terrorists killed a second hostage, sixty-four-year-old Dr Heinz Hillegart. The Swedes then decided to attack; but, before they could do so, the terrorists made a bungled attempt to blow up the building, wounding all the hostages and killing two of themselves. The other four were arrested, returned to Germany and imprisoned.

Eight months later two members of the RAF took part, under the command of Carlos, in the kidnapping of the OPEC oil ministers in Vienna; and in 1976, two more of them led the hijacking of the French aircraft to Entebbe, where both of them and most of their Palestinian comrades were reportedly killed in the rescue of the passengers by the Israeli commandos.

In November 1976 a West German traffic patrol arrested a thirty-two-year-old lawyer, Siegfried Haag, in possession of a pistol, forged passports and banknotes traced to two bank robberies, together with what police believed to be a coded 'hit list' of leading public figures in Germany. He had been Baader's lawyer and had regularly visited him in prison from 1972 to 1975. He had been arrested before, in May 1975, on suspicion of smuggling arms and acting as a courier between the first-generation members in prison and the second-generation ones outside; but on that occasion the charges were dropped. He had thereupon quit his law practice and gone underground, allegedly telling Baader that what he could not do in the courts he would do with the gun. In 1975 and 1976 he recruited thirty new members for the RAF. He was believed to have planned the raid on the German embassy in Stockholm, and possibly also the operations carried out by the third generation in 1977. The death or capture of eight RAF terrorists at Stockholm and Entebbe, and the arrest of Haag in November 1976, effectively mark the end of the second generation.

Though most of the first and second generations are dead or in prison, they remain important because their myth, and the 'martyrdom' of those who killed themselves in prison still exerts great influence on their successors; and also because their origins and life histories, now well documented, contribute much to our understanding of the third generation and their remaining supporters—and also of the Red Brigades in Italy (see below).

In the period from 1968 to 1972, the heyday of the anti-Vietnam demonstrations in American and European universities, it is estimated that more than 100,000 German students sympathised, more or less openly, with the aims and activities of Ennslin, Baader and Meinhof. Most of these were the sons and daughters of middle-class parents—as, of course, were the Baader-Meinhof group themselves. This is the case everywhere:

in the USA, Japan and Europe; and one of the reasons may be that middle-class students have a subconscious confidence in three 'safety nets' which their fellow students from poorer backgrounds do not have. Those safety nets are: confidence that they can always get a job; that they can play the social security game; or that they can, if need be, fall back on prosperous families who will forgive and maintain them. The sons or daughters of working-class parents, having worked hard to get better prospects, have no wish to throw them all away or to betray the sacrifices their parents are making for them (or to break their hearts), so they continue working hard at university and seldom get involved in revolutionary politics.

In the late 1960s and early 1970s most 'revolutionary students' in Germany—as elsewhere—went after graduation into jobs where they could use their brains, possibly hoping still to exert radical influence as, for example, journalists, teachers or lawyers. A few, however, (perhaps about 1 per cent in 1970, declining to less than 1,000 by 1976) worked on the fringes of violent revolutionary movements, either 'dropping out of the rat race' to live in communes or squats, or doing normal jobs and discreetly providing safe houses, cars, etc., for those who did the killing. Some drifted into, or returned to, this semi-clandestine or clandestine life in their thirties or even forties (for example Meinhof and Haag), sometimes continuing to work as journalists, teachers or lawyers.

Of these semi-clandestine 1,000 or so, some went on to become active terrorists, perhaps totalling fifty or sixty at any one time, new ones replacing old ones who dropped out or were killed or arrested. They seldom seemed to start killing until their middle twenties or later, and more than half were women.

The same applies to the third generation. Of the forty-four on the wanted list at the end of 1977, twenty-three (53 per cent) had been to university, though most of them dropped out. Another seven (16 per cent) had qualified for university (*Abitur*) but did not go. Ten (23 per cent) went to technical college, and only four (9 per cent) were manual workers. The forty-four had an average age of twenty-eight, and twenty-five of them (57 per cent) were women.

The second generation's cold-blooded killing (e.g. of Judge

Drenkmann and the two hostages in Stockholm) began to alienate their student sympathizers, even though 4,000 attended Ulrike Meinhof's funeral after her suicide in 1976. After Entebbe, as the second generation passed into the third, the killing became even more clinically professional. Public Prosecutor Siegfried Buback was shot dead in his car by two terrorists on motorcycles in April 1977. The well secured home of Jürgen Ponto, Chairman of the Dresdner Bank, was penetrated in July 1977 by the treachery of a twenty-six-year-old girl, Susanne Albrecht, who was known and accepted as a family friend: she was Ponto's goddaughter. She bore a gift of flowers—'It's me, Susanne'—and the door was opened to her. She and her comrades probably intended to kidnap Jürgen Ponto; but when he resisted, they shot him dead.

In September 1977 the RAF kidnapped and later killed the President of the West German Employers' and Industrial Association, Dr Hanns-Martin Schleyer (this kidnapping will be described more fully in Chapter Fifteen). During the kidnap they killed Schleyer's driver and his escort of three policemen, and television pictures of their working-class families weeping at their funerals still further alienated public sympathy from the RAF, including that of student radicals.

The third generation appeared to care little for public support, either from the semi-clandestine fringes, or from the open radical left. Some of their committed lawyers continued to help them, especially in using prison visits to their clients to maintain contact with the first and second generations; but from 1977 the RAF terrorists generally preferred to rely only on their fellow members of the hard core—though these might be expected to prove their worth in auxiliary tasks before being entrusted with the actual killing or kidnapping. It is significant (see Chapter Fifteen) that when flats were rented in advance as hideouts for the Hanns-Martin Schleyer kidnapping, the people doing so were all on the wanted list for previous murders or kidnappings (they used false names), and not, as would have happened previously, unsuspected volunteers from the fringe supporters.

At the end of 1977, student radicals were increasingly deserting the RAF for a new political movement: the Revolutionary Cells, whose newspaper *Revolutionärer Zorn* ('revolutionary anger') urged its members not to risk killing anyone; their philosophy was to bomb the symbols of capitalism (shops, ticket machines etc.), mainly at night to avoid casualties. This, of course, was where Ennslin and Baader had begun in 1968. It remains to be seen whether this generation of German radical students will hold to their present view that killing is counterproductive, or whether they are merely starting a new cycle, which will escalate and produce a fourth and fifth generation of even more lethal terrorists.

The RAF are certainly not short of money. Much of their wealth has been acquired by criminal kidnapping for ransom. There have been at least fifty criminal kidnappings in Germany in the past five years, and some of these have undoubtedly been done by or on behalf of the RAF. They were involved in three particularly lucrative kidnappings in December 1977, after the murder of Dr Schleyer. Two of these were in Vienna (Lotte Böhm and Walter Michael Palmers), and the third in Munich (Richard Oetker). The total ransoms for these three amounted to over $12 million, of which it is likely that the lion's share went to the RAF. Gabriele Kröcher-Tiedemann (one of the women released in exchange for Peter Lorenz in 1975, and also wanted for murder in the OPEC kidnapping in Vienna later that year) was arrested in Switzerland in January 1978, on her way to Italy, with about $200,000 from the Palmers ransom. This illustrates both the financial and international aspects of RAF operations.

THE ITALIAN ENVIRONMENT

Most of the seventy-six recorded kidnappings in Italy in 1977 were by criminal gangs for ransom, with only rare, and usually uncertain, contacts with political groups. A senior police officer in Milan estimated that 80 per cent were carried out by or on behalf of the Mafia by Italians from Calabria, Sardinia or Sicily, 15 per cent by small-time criminals and only 5 per cent by political groups,[1] though some of these, like that of ex-Prime Minister Aldo Moro, were highly sensational.

Italy has a strong tradition of criminal violence and a weak

1. *New York Times Magazine*, 20th November 1977.

tradition of democracy. Its electoral system, unlike the German one, has produced a series of short-lived governments, relying on compromise with splinter parties rather than on a coalition of two. The Christian Democratic Party, having continually headed these governments, is saddled with responsibility for their shortcomings.

The orthodox Communist Party (PCI), paradoxically, is the strongest in its demands for law and order and, where it holds power in local government (Rome, Naples and Bologna all have Communist mayors), it is more effective than others in maintaining it. Representing manual workers, now relatively affluent by past Italian standards, the PCI has little sympathy with either the rich Mafia gangs or with political extremists of right or left. This, coupled with its decision to co-operate with the minority Christian Democrat government from 1976 to 1978, has infuriated the far left. Radical students and graduates are cynical about the prospects of political change through the democratic process and, like Ennslin, Baader and Meinhof in Germany, have turned in frustration to the gun, mainly in the Red Brigades who, with associated movements, were credited up to the end of 1977 with as many as 100 kidnaps and murders—compared with twenty-four murders by the Red Army Fraction in Germany.

Their frustration is compounded by the Italian educational system, which guarantees anyone of even mediocre academic attainment the right to study at university for as many years as he likes. As a result, most Italian universities have up to eight times as many students as they were designed to take. Enrolment in 1977 was 800,000 and of those only 9 per cent (71,000) completed a degree in that year—less than half the number one would expect in any one year. Lectures are overcrowded and chaotic, and often disrupted by heckling. The kind of personal tutorial supervision used in British universities is almost unknown. Even those who do graduate find it difficult to get jobs, and the student image created by the Red Brigades does not help. Maturing revolutionaries find in universities a fertile field for their politics; and they themselves can stay on as 'students', working part time, almost indefinitely.

THE RED BRIGADES

Despite the fundamental contrasts between Italy and Germany—politically, socially, economically and in terms of efficiency of the police and intelligence services—there has been a remarkable similarity in the pattern of development of the Italian Red Brigades and the German Red Army Fraction. This must be due largely to their both being based upon the same Marxist-Leninist (Marcusian) philosophies, as expounded in universities where there is constant exchange of students from different countries.

The Red Brigades were founded by Renato Curcio, at that time twenty-eight years old, who had earlier propounded the idea of a 'negative university', initially at Trento University, where he was a sociology student.

It was a parallel movement, the Partisan Action Groups (GAP), which began terrorist violence in 1970. GAP was led by a rich young publisher, Giangiacomo Feltrinelli who, with his wife, was a friend of Ulrike Meinhof and contributed to the RAF. Feltrinelli was mysteriously killed in an incident in which a pylon was blown up in Northern Italy in 1972. After his death, GAP members (about fifty, of whom ten were hardcore terrorists) joined Curcio's Red Brigades, which then turned more to violence.

For the next three years there was a series of attacks, mainly on industry, with the aim of exacerbating relations between management and labour. Their slogans were 'Bite and run' and 'Strike one to educate a hundred.' The principal victims were junior managers and supervisors, who were beaten up, had their cars burned, or were temporarily kidnapped (to secure immediate local concessions) but not killed.

From April 1972 they turned to more clandestine violence, declaring war, as they put it, 'on the heart of the state': selecting their targets from the managerial world, the Christian Democrat Party and the judiciary, the police and the prisons. In 1974 they kidnapped Judge Sossi, demanding the release of six Red Brig-

2. Jillian Becker, *Hitler's Children* (Panther, London, 1978).

ades prisoners. The government stood firm and Sossi was released, having signed a 'confession', after forty-four days in captivity.

By 1974, the Red Brigades contained two factions: a militant one which believed in killing, and a more moderate one (led by Curcio) which did not. In 1974, the militant faction raided a club of the right-wing parliamentary political party *Movimento Sociale Italiano* (MSI) in Padua and killed two of its members. The moderate leadership were critical, and for a time they prevailed. In October 1974, however, Curcio and others were arrested, and the militant faction gradually took over the leadership.

There was a period of reorganization from 1974 to 1976, in which a disciplined cell organization was developed. Security was strict, with only one cell member having contact with superior or subordinate cells. The 'red brigades' themselves, despite their name, were just the basic cells, each four or five strong, whose task was to organize local collaborators on the fringes, who would in turn recruit and indoctrinate students and others from the large pool of sympathizers in the universities. Three or four such brigades (cells) were co-ordinated by a 'column' with responsibility for one city or region, and the columns were responsible to a national headquarters giving strategic direction. The total strength of this cell structure of the Red Brigades— HQ, columns and brigades—was in 1978 estimated at 150 to 200.

As in Germany, there was a fringe of semi-clandestine active supporters, some opting out of society to live in communes or squats, and others giving part-time support whilst working as journalists, lawyers, teachers etc. These numbered about 2,000 in 1978—a great many more than in Germany in that year, though similar to the number a few years earlier.

The pool of sympathizers, mainly in the universities, was far larger than in Germany: about 150,000 in 1978. These, known as the *Autonomia Operaia* ('workers' autonomy'), were the demonstrators (violent or otherwise) who disrupted the life of the cities and universities and provided the pool from which all the left-wing extremists recruited, not only the Red Brigades, but also the Armed Proletarian Nuclei (NAP—closely associated with the Red Brigades), the *Gruppi Armati Clandestini Prima Linea* ('underground front-line armed groups'), and anything up to 200 other movements which sprouted, blossomed, faded and died,

as in other countries, but on a far larger and more bewildering
scale. As the PCI co-operates increasingly in parliamentary
government, there may be a tendency of more left-wing movements to gather around the rival party, the *Partito Communista
Marxista Leninista* (PCML), which is sometimes called Maoist
but, like its British and other parallels, is really an élitist, anti-
parliamentary party organized on Leninist-Stalinist lines. If this
happens, it would probably make the violence (whether greater
or less) more efficient, and closely directed to political ends.

The number of extreme right-wing groups is fewer; but some
are as tightly organized and as violent as the Red Brigades,
though on a smaller scale.

Political violence in Italy has been on a horrifying scale. Since
1969, political extremists of the right and left have made more
than 8,000 violent attacks, killing more than eighty and wounding
over 500. In 1977 the number killed and wounded by politically
motivated shootings rose sharply to forty-eight. In the same year
over 120 attacks were made on Christian Democratic party
offices, nearly 100 on those of the MSI, and fifty-eight on those
of the PCI. The police hold about 300 right-wing suspects
(mostly arrested before 1976) and a similar number of left-wing
suspects (148 from the Red Brigades, 126 from NAP and fourteen
from Front Line). Judicial proceedings can be delayed almost
indefinitely on points of law. As one example, the trial of those
accused of killing sixteen people in a bomb attack in Milan in
1969 did not begin until 1978.[3]

The Red Brigades have concentrated especially on delaying the
trial in Turin of fourteen of their members (including Curcio)
by violent intimidation of judges, lawyers, witnesses and jurors.
The trial was postponed in 1976 by the murder of the Genoa
Prosecutor General; again in May 1977 by the murder of a
defence lawyer; and then yet again in March 1978 by the killing
of a police officer who had led an anti-terrorist team. Numerous
others have been 'kneecapped',[4] and both lawyers and jurors
have constantly sought excuses for not attending the court.

3. These and many other facts can be found in a survey of Italy in
   The Economist, 1st April 1978.
4. Shot in the knees; but among the IRA this crippling punishment
   is often administered with a power drill.

At the same time, the Red Brigades have shot or kneecapped large numbers of other lawyers, journalists and industrialists, as always including a majority of junior managers. In the first three months of 1977 they killed six people by shooting, including a bank manager and a magistrate.

Their most sensational operation was the kidnapping on 16th March 1978 of Aldo Moro, six times Prime Minister, tipped as the next President. He was, ironically, the Christian Democratic politician who had done most of all to work for reconciliation with the left, and also to restrict the powers of the police and intelligence services in dealing with political violence.

The kidnapping itself—in which five bodyguards were killed—followed a very similar pattern to that of Dr Hanns-Martin Schleyer, and there were suggestions that RAF members may have been involved. The kidnappers demanded the release of Curcio and his fellow Red Brigades prisoners.

Television pictures of the tearful working-class families of the murdered guards drew widespread public anger, even amongst Red Brigades student sympathizers. The PCI and trade union members were disgusted at middle-class revolutionaries claiming to act in the name of the working class and Communism. The government stood firm and with PCI support passed rapid legislation to strengthen the powers of the police for arrest, interrogation, searching and tapping of telephones and for immediate registration of purchase or renting of accommodation. Massive police deployment caused a slump in other forms of crime, but all was to no avail.

The kidnappers treated Moro like children who take off the wings of a butterfly and watch it wriggle to death. He was made to write humiliating letters to his family and colleagues. The government was also humiliated when, for example, they reacted to a report that Moro's body had been dumped in a frozen mountain lake. He was eventually killed after fifty-five days in captivity.

The other aim of provoking over-reaction initially seemed to fail. In subsequent local elections the authoritarian parties of left and right (the PCI and MSI) both lost ground. The kidnapping did, however, goad all parties into facing up to the shortcomings of the police and intelligence services (see below).

ITALIAN CRIMINALS AND THE POLICE

There is in Italy a particularly bewildering overlap between criminal and political terrorists (as earlier described on pages 39–40), some of the smaller groups often engaging criminal gangs to do their work for them. Even allowing for this, however, at least 95 per cent, and possibly as many as 98 per cent, of the kidnappings in Italy are purely for criminal gain. Ransoms have in five years reached a total of about 100 billion lire ($120 million). There were sixty-three kidnappings reported in 1975, forty-eight in 1976 and seventy-six in 1977. These amounted to more than 75 per cent of all the known kidnappings in Europe. The victims (in contrast to those in Latin America) have seldom been expatriates, but have mostly been Italian industrialists, bankers and merchants or, increasingly, their children—and even the children of farmers in small villages, whose inhabitants are required to club together to find a ransom which the kidnappers believe to be within their collective resources. There are many more extortions under the threat of kidnapping and these are often paid without being reported.

The police in Italy have unrivalled experience in handling violent crime. There are, however, three separate 'police forces'. The Carabinieri (80,000) are a branch of the armed forces under the Defence Ministry, and were originally formed for operation in rural areas with a nationwide responsibility for law and order. The Police (also 80,000) were intended to be responsible for urban areas, and come under the control of the Ministry of the Interior. Over the years, the spread of the cities and the urbanization of villages has obscured this demarcation and, in practice, both now have a nationwide deployment and their responsibilities for law and order overlap. Then there are the Fiscal Police (40,000), controlled by the Ministry of Finance, who counter fraud, tax evasion and smuggling. The Fiscal Police become involved in kidnapping mainly in two ways: in monitoring the gathering (and tracing) of currency for ransom; and in detecting fraudulent kidnaps and ransoms.

When there is a kidnap, an examining magistrate is appointed to co-ordinate the activities of the various police forces. Whichever of the Police or the Carabinieri are first to arrive on the scene of the kidnap normally takes charge of the case, but the examining magistrate can either confirm or reverse this as he judges fit. The existence of two wholly separate forces does, however, mean that many useful intelligence sources may be excluded, since each has its own. Intelligence contacts with criminal gangs (including the Mafia) are plentiful, but these in themselves offer temptations for corruption or connivance. There is also great scope for misunderstanding—as, for example, in January 1978, when the leader of a Calabrian Mafia group responsible for a large number of kidnaps in Milan was shot dead by a Police patrol whilst talking to a plain-clothes member of the Carabinieri, who was also wounded. Similar problems arise over the co-ordination of investigation.

Intelligence has been further weakened by the truncation of the government security services (and compromising of some of their sources) by Christian Democrat leaders lacking a parliamentary majority, trying to placate liberal or left-wing politicians in their search for partners in coalitions, or for support in the House for other difficult legislation.

Because of the high level of crime and political violence, and the weaknesses in intelligence and co-ordination, the casualties amongst police and Carabinieri have been high, and none can feel that they or their families are wholly safe from assassination. This intimidation further increases the temptations of corruption or connivance.

There have also been a number of cases of fraud and tax fiddling. Some magistrates have tried to freeze assets or the release of currency from banks, or to make the payment of ransoms in other ways illegal. This has, in practice, often driven the victim's family to find ways of settling quickly and secretly, without co-operating with the police—to the detriment of the opportunities for detection and arrest of the kidnappers.

Considering all these difficulties, the detection rate for kidnapping is not bad. In 1975, for example, 133 people were arrested in twenty-seven of the sixty-three cases reported to the police. Nevertheless, the overall percentage of convictions for kidnapping is far lower than in the USA (90 per cent), as well as in most European countries; and this is of great encouragement to the gangs which specialize in this crime. On the other hand, the Police and Carabinieri themselves had occasion for encouragement in April 1978, when they arrested two kidnappers in the act of collecting a ransom for sixteen-year-old Michela Marconi. The interrogation enabled them to raid the hideout and rescue the girl. It also enabled them to ambush another gang of the same group, who were moving a second hostage, Angelo Apolloni, to a new hideout, and he too was rescued.

Some examples of kidnapping in Italy are given in Chapter Sixteen.

OTHER CRIMINAL AND POLITICAL TERRORISTS IN EUROPE

There are active political terrorist movements in virtually every other European country; and there is some co-operation between them, usually on a casual basis. The IRA, for example, is known to have had contacts with the Basque separatists (ETA) in Spain, and with the Breton Liberation Front (FLB) in France. There are also several Corsican separatist movements; and the German Red Army Fraction has clearly found collaborators and safe houses in France and the Netherlands, and probably also in Belgium, Luxembourg and Italy. The kidnapping in France of M Revelli-Beaumont in 1977 appears to have been done by Latin Americans (see page 55). The Dutch have the Rode Hulf, a small movement similar in philosophy to the RAF, which also collaborates with the Japanese and Palestinian terrorists. The South Moluccans, however, appear to have no international contacts, and their mass kidnappings have aimed mainly for publicity. There are some case studies of kidnapping in the Netherlands in Chapter Thirteen.

Spain and Portugal, only recently emerging from authoritarian rule, each have a large number of extreme left- and right-wing movements. So have Greece and Turkey. The *Annual of Power and Conflict* (published by the Institute for the Study of Conflict, London) provides the most convenient guide to these movements.

As in Italy, there is overlap and co-operation between criminal and political organizations.

The most sensational of recent criminal kidnappings in Western Europe was that of the Belgian Baron Empain in France in 1978; and this provides an illustration both of a small but professional criminal gang in action, and of co-operation between the police and the family in saving the victim and arresting at least some of the criminals. There is a brief case study of it in Chapter Fourteen.

Chapter Three

North and South Americans and others

THE PALESTINIANS

ONLY one Palestinian group has regularly carried out terrorist operations outside the Middle East: the Popular Front for the Liberation of Palestine (PFLP). Two others have engaged in occasional actions. The Black September Organization, which was in fact a code name for members of Yasser Arafat's al-Fatah, brought off a number of spectacular operations between 1971 and 1974, including the kidnapping of Israeli athletes at the Munich Olympics in 1972. And members of the Syrian-based Saiqa (who also used a one-off codename: 'Eagles of the Palestinian Revolution') kidnapped two Russian Jews en route for Israel and an Austrian official to force the Austrian Government to close the Schonau transit camp in 1973.

The PFLP's terrorist operations were mainly organized by Dr Wadi Haddad until he died in 1978. The PFLP leader, Dr George Habash, claimed that Haddad had broken away to form an independent group in 1972. The total strength of the PFLP is about 500, and most of these are based in refugee camps (or more accurately in blocks of refugee flats) in Lebanon, though Haddad was based in Iraq, where he ran a training camp for his terrorist squads. PFLP also runs branches in many other countries, including some in Europe, and has regular and effective operating links with other movements, notably the Japanese Red Army and the West German Red Army Fraction (see below). The PFLP is extremely rich, getting its funds partly from ransoms (paid mainly for the release of hijacked aircraft) but mainly from Arab oil states, some willingly (notably Libya, Algeria and

Iraq) and others under coercion, in the form of protection money under threat of destruction of their oil installations or the kidnapping and murder of their ministers. The kidnapping in 1975 of the eleven OPEC oil ministers, including those of Saudi Arabia and Iran, both unsympathetic to the PFLP, is believed to have brought them a ransom of $25 million.

CARLOS AND THE PFLP EUROPEAN COMMANDO

Ilyich Ramirez Sanchez ('Carlos') was the son of a Venezuelan Marxist millionaire who called his sons Vladimir, Ilyich and Lenin. Carlos studied at the Lumumba University in Moscow, from which he was expelled in 1969. This expulsion is considered by some to have been a blind, but it was probably genuine. Carlos's political views do seem far apart from orthodox Russian Communism—though this would not stop the KGB from giving him practical assistance in operations which would embarrass, weaken or divide the Western democracies or the conservative oil states.

Carlos went to Jordan in 1970, and joined the PFLP in their fight against King Hussein. After a spell as a 'sleeper' in London he took command of the PFLP European Commando, after its leader (Mohammed Boudia) had been killed by an Israeli hit squad in June 1973. The Commando was based in Paris but Carlos maintained his contacts in London. He did a number of rather ineffective operations, including the attempted murder of Edward Sieff, head of Marks and Spencer, in December 1973, and two abortive attacks on Israeli aircraft at Orly Airport in January 1975, before shooting his way out of arrest by the Paris police in June 1975. He reappeared to lead the OPEC kidnapping in Vienna in December 1975, in which he positively sought exposure on world television. Since then—probably because his face is now so well known—he has operated as an organizer, planner and trainer, supposedly moving between Libya, Algeria and Aden.

Much was learned about his life as leader of the PFLP European Commando as a result of the attempt to arrest him in Paris, and the subsequent searches of his safe houses in London. He had four girlfriends, two in each city, who gave him keys to their flats, where they allowed him to keep locked suitcases containing (probably unknown to the girls) guns and explosives. Travelling as an apparently prosperous Latin American salesman, on various forged passports, he would go direct from the airport to let himself into one of these flats, sometimes having previously written to the girl to have local currency, etc., ready for him. He could thus perform his operations without the need to smuggle anything suspicious, and could rely on a warm bed for the night. It was a good life. Most of the girls later paid for being duped by serving a few months in gaol.

Carlos received his orders through a PFLP courier from Beirut, Michael Moukharbel, who betrayed him and led the Paris police to Carlos' current flat (Carlos shot Moukharbel dead along with two of the policemen). The cell in Paris probably contained less than a dozen members (not including the witting or unwitting auxiliaries like the girls), but it directed the work of other cells and couriers all over Europe. During Boudia's time it had conducted operations in Germany, Holland and Italy. Most of the members were probably Arabs or Latin Americans working or studying in Europe. Like the Irish immigrants who manned the ASU, they seem to have lived normal, open lives (Boudia, a cultured, French-speaking Algerian, was the administrative director of a Paris theatre). Such groups are not easy to detect.

THE JAPANESE RED ARMY

The Japanese Red Army (JRA) is probably the most violent and fanatical of all terrorist movements, and has worked in close co-operation with the PFLP and the German Red Army Fraction, and also with Carlos.

The JRA was formed in 1969 by militant students frustrated by Japan's apparently unshakeable economic growth and political stability, and disillusioned by the impotence of student rioters in 1968 in Europe and the USA. After a number of bizarre and largely abortive operations, five of them were captured in a police raid on a mountain training camp in February 1972. Interrogation revealed the ruthlessness of their training, and led to the discovery of the bodies of fourteen of their comrades, who had been stripped and tied up to freeze to death in the snow for showing 'bourgeois tendencies'.

Later, on 30th May 1972, three members of the JRA carried out the Lod Airport massacre. These three had been trained in North Korea; had offered their services to the PFLP; and had moved for final training and briefing to Lebanon, thence to Frankfurt to collect forged passports, and to Rome to pick up suitcases containing Czech weapons and grenades. They then boarded an Air France aircraft for Lod Airport; on arrival they drew out their weapons in the baggage hall, and killed twenty-six people and wounded seventy-two—mainly, by chance, Puerto Rican pilgrims on their way to Bethlehem. This operation illustrates not only the ruthlessness but also the international nature of the JRA.

Other JRA operations have included a combined hijacking and kidnapping operation extending from Singapore to Kuwait; and the seizure of hostages at the French Embassy at the Hague in 1974, in conjunction with the PFLP and Carlos, in order to secure the release of one of their comrades held by the French. Their most successful operation to date has been the hijacking of a Japanese aircraft on 28th September 1977, for which the Japanese government flew five JRA prisoners to Aden with a ransom of $6 million.

The JRA have thus far operated in very small groups, usually based upon resident cell organizations in the target countries, such as the PFLP European Commando or the German Red Army Fraction. Their members contribute an extreme degree of ruthlessness and (when under siege) of resistance to fear or persuasion, and are trained to stifle the emergence of the traces of human sympathy towards their hostages which many other terrorists eventually display.

THE USA AND CANADA

The success of the US police and FBI in arresting criminal kidnappers was described in the Introduction. In a country with a very high homicide rate, this is a remarkable achievement, and has proved an effective deterrent.

This may also be a reason why political terrorists in the USA have done much more bombing and shooting than kidnapping. This could easily have been otherwise, since the revolutionary student movements, such as those already described in Germany and Italy, really began in the USA, first under the impetus of the Civil Rights movement, and from 1967 as a protest against US involvement in Vietnam. The anti-Vietnam movement spread, via American students, into European and Japanese universities, and provided the focus for the wave of violent protest in 1968 which escalated into lethal terrorist violence.

The US 'Students for a Democratic Society' (SDS) gave birth to the Weathermen, who set off over 4,000 bombs in 1969 and 1970, mainly (like those in Germany) intended to destroy property rather than lives. As elsewhere, the bombers were almost all university-educated. Later another group of radicals, mainly students or graduates from the University of California in Berkeley, attempted a 'symbiosis' of intellectuals and deprived criminals in the Symbionese Liberation Army which, after one murder of a black education official, kidnapped a millionaire's daughter, Patty Hearst. She was amongst the first to illustrate the phenomenon of a hostage succumbing to the psychological dependence on her captors, later taking part in an armed robbery with them. As usual in the USA, all her kidnappers have been either killed or arrested and convicted.

Political kidnappings, however, remain exceptional, whilst criminal kidnappings seem to have increased since 1974, along with other types of crime in the USA. In 1975, for example, 226 kidnapping cases were reported, and in 1976 another 206. Political extremists, such as the Black Liberation Movement, The New World Liberation Front and the Weather Underground, continue to concentrate on bombing, and over recent years have caused on average six or seven bombings per month, mostly without fatal casualties.

In Canada there have also been more criminal than political kidnappings. In 1970 separate cells of the Quebec Liberation Front (FLQ) carried out two sensational kidnappings, the first of a Quebec minister (whom they killed) and the second of a British diplomat. The Trudeau government, however, reacted strongly, and public hostility to the FLQ was so intense that the movement went into abeyance; even legitimate Quebec separatism was discredited for the next five years. The strength of the government's reaction, however, caused the survivors of the movement to harbour a bitter resolve for revenge. Political activity revived in the mid-1970s, and a separatist provincial government was elected in Quebec. If separatism is frustrated, by federal opposition, by insufficient public support or otherwise, terrorism in Canada could reappear.

LATIN-AMERICAN TERRORISTS

Terrorist organizations have been far more numerous, and far bigger, in Latin America than anywhere else in the world. They include right-wing and left-wing groups, which fight each other; and in some countries some of these undoubtedly work in collusion with the police.

Amongst the more active right-wing groups are the AAA in Argentina, the Death Squads in Brazil, the UGB in El Salvador and MANO in Guatemala. The most active left-wing groups include the ERP and the Monteneros in Argentina, the ELN in Colombia, the FAR in Guatemala and the FALN in Venezuela. Other groups, very active in the past, had largely been rendered inactive by 1977 by intensive military operations; these include the ELN in Bolivia, the ALN and VPR in Brazil, the MIR in Chile and the Tupamaros in Uruguay.[1]

Latin-American groups, though they have sometimes operated with limited success in rural areas, are mainly urban-based, and recruited from a very large pool of middle-class students and graduates, who are frustrated by the lack of job opportunities commensurate with their education. In Argentina they have been joined by a substantial number of militant workers, equally frustrated by the strong, conservative trade unions.

1. Readers with a particular interest in Latin America would be wise to refer to the current edition of *The Annual of Power and Conflict* (Institute for the Study of Conflict, London), which catalogues all these movements (and others throughout the world) in detail. For an excellent analysis of the origins and motivations of Latin-American terrorist groups see Ernst Halperin, *Terrorism in Latin America* (Sage Publications, Beverly Hills and London, 1976).

The terrorists and their supporters most commonly live double lives, and are based in ordinary homes and flats in the suburbs. As an indication of the contrast in scale with other parts of the world, the Tupamaros at their peak in 1970 numbered about 3,000. In 1973–4 there were believed to be over 10,000 guerrillas operating in Argentina, of whom perhaps 2,000 were in armed 'fire groups' (each normally about five strong), and the remainder in supporting cells. The organization and tasks of these cells are further discussed in Chapter Four.

By 1977, these numbers had been drastically eroded by the military regimes which their activities had helped to create. Thousands of them fled their countries and sought employment or places at universities (many of their families were rich) in Europe, especially in Spain and Italy. Most, no doubt, had had their fill of revolutionary life, but others (mainly from Argentina and Chile) formed an organization known as the Junta de Coordinación Revolucionaria (JCR) with its headquarters in Paris, and with cells in most other European capitals. They organized training for their members in Cuba, Libya and Iraq, and with the Cubans in Africa; and issued training manuals for their members in the use of weapons and explosives, guerrilla tactics, communication, the organization of subversion and propaganda, and the forgery of documents.

Thus far (1978) they have been mainly in an organization phase. They communicate through the legitimate channels of the Association of Latin-American Students, and concentrate on raising money, on developing their cell structure, on political discussion, study and training, and on the establishment of contacts with European and Palestinian sympathizers, both in revolutionary movements and amongst journalists, teachers and lawyers.

There are, however, signs of increasing involvement of Latin Americans in European kidnappings. In July 1977, for example, nine South Americans (including seven Argentinians) were arrested after the kidnapping of M Revelli-Beaumont, head of the French Fiat subsidiary, who was ransomed for $2 million after being held for seventy days. (It is significant that the Monteneros had planned to kidnap M Revelli-Beaumont when he had been head of Fiat in Argentina, and had already kidnapped or murdered several other Fiat executives there.)

The Latin-American emigré terrorists may have access to huge balances in European banks from past operations (see page 17). With the spread of their expertise, it may be that the time for which hostages are held will be longer, and the size of ransom demands increased. Co-operation by German and Latin-American terrorists, with their two brands of professionalism, as described in the case studies in Part III of this book, could be a particularly dangerous combination.

Chapter Four

Terrorist Tactics and Techniques

ORGANIZATION FOR KIDNAPPING

A kidnapping may be carried out by a group of any size, criminal or political, ranging from a large international organization to a single cell or even (particularly if the victim is a young girl or small child to whom no threat is suspected) by a single criminal.

Political terrorists are likely to operate in small cells, ranging from a handful of amateurs to a multicellular organization hundreds or thousands strong. These cells may vary in type, and not all will necessarily be armed. There will be armed fire groups, usually four or five strong. There may be any number of auxiliary cells to organize such things as safe houses, 'prisons' (often in cellars under these houses), transport, communications, publicity, intelligence networks and robberies and extortions for party funds. And there may be more open political cells, which recruit and vet probationers for graduation later to the auxiliary cells and fire groups; these political cells will also carry out overt fund raising, run the party newspaper, organize demonstrations and prepare and distribute propaganda.

In the larger movements there is likely to be a superior cell for command and control. If they are well organized, only one member of each subordinate cell (or system of cells) will have contact with this command and control HQ, and members of different cells should not know each other. In movements several thousands strong, as in some Latin-American countries, there will be structures like the above in various districts, each having clearly defined areas of operation, with a higher command hierarchy above them.

The kidnapping of a public figure, such as an executive of a large corporation, or of a member of his family, is more likely to be attempted by one of the larger organizations, whether criminal or political. They may deploy a number of teams with different responsibilities, and which have little or no direct contact with each other: one for the snatch itself; three or four others to cause diversions and block traffic intersections; possibly another ready to transfer the victim to a different vehicle for transport to the hideout; a team to guard him (or two or three in shifts); one to handle the negotiations; another for the publicity and propaganda; and yet another for the communications; and there will in such a case certainly be a superior cell for overall command and control.

As an example of this, when the Tupamaros in 1971 kidnapped the British ambassador in Uruguay, Geoffrey (now Sir Geoffrey) Jackson, the snatch was done in the centre of Montevideo, close to his embassy, when the narrow streets were normally full of traffic. Multiple teams were deployed and co-ordinated (presumably by radio) to block every intersection leading on to the planned escape route. He was initially driven away in his own car, but was soon afterwards transferred to a van waiting at a pre-arranged spot. This was driven into some kind of covered garage or shed with access to the cellar where he was to be held. Here he was guarded by teams of three, each for three weeks on end, comprising in all some thirty Tupamaros. Someone else was handling propaganda, which included visits by two left-wing journalists for interviews with him. Another group came later with a vehicle to move him to a new hideout, and another eventually to take him away to be released. Though all wore hoods (after the initial snatch) his impression was that he very rarely met the same person in more than one of these roles, and that on those occasions it was probably someone higher in the hierarchy.[1]

Preparation and Reconnaissance

The terrorists' most important decision is the selection of their

1. See Geoffrey Jackson, *People's Prison* (Faber and Faber, London, 1972); also published as *Surviving the Long Night* (Vanguard, New York, 1974).

victim. In most cases the primary factors are whether he (or she, his family, or his firm, are rich enough to find a large ransom; and how willing they are likely to be to pay. The character of other members of the family or firm may also be a consideration. There is at least one group in Latin America which specifies that the selected victim must have a determined and articulate wife who will apply pressure on his firm to pay for his release.

Other factors are the victim's vulnerability: his lifestyle and the publicity attached to it; the predictability of his movements; his attitude to precautions and security; and his protection at home, at work and on the move. In a political kidnapping, the prospects for publicity, and the potential leverage on the government, will be important; and other factors, such as revenge and the extraction of information, may also apply.

Professionally organized kidnap groups will carry out detailed research into the potential victim's background, character and health, and his strong and weak points. They will also study his movements and security, and build up a dossier of his family, friends, business associates, legal advisers and others whom they think might prove useful during negotiation. In all of these things they may be helped by material in directories and trade publications and by press reports of the victim's life and of his engagements.

This will be followed by thorough reconnaissance, first to select an occasion for the snatch, and then to examine the chosen site in detail, together with the habits of guards and security men involved. In the case of a kidnap on the road, test runs may be made, monitoring the victim's journey to and from work.

Before he was kidnapped, Geoffrey Jackson became aware that, in a park across the street from his house, there always seemed to be a young couple with a baby having a picnic—different couples but following the same pattern—and watching his comings and goings with interest. On the road to work, he noticed that a scooter frequently cut in front of his car, always carrying a young man and a girl, different people but with the same scooter with the same registration number. Sometimes a car or van would do what seemed to be a dummy run to decide how best it might cut in to block his car at possible snatch points. And outside the embassy he saw a pair of students 'canoodling', but apparently more interested in him than in each other. They too had a scooter, whose number was traced to a student with known Tupamaro sympathies. After the snatch itself, he caught sight of a face he had seen before in one of the reconnaissance runs—a brief identification before the hoods blacked out the faces.[2]

An example of the thought given to reconnaissance and planning by a sophisticated political terrorist organization in Argentina is given in Chapter Seventeen.

THE SNATCH

Over 90 per cent of kidnappings occur when the victim is in his car on the way to or from work, fairly close to either his home or his office, where it may be difficult for him to vary his route, even if he is able to vary the time or the type of car he uses. Narrow streets are more often chosen than broad ones, where a trained driver can take evasive action.

A typical plan is as follows. A pair of observers report the victim's departure from his home or office, perhaps from a nearby telephone box, or by radio from a parked car, or from a café or bar overlooking the gate. Other observers are ready to signal the entry of the victim's car into the selected street, upon which a blockage is created by a staged 'accident', or by a van stalling its engine while turning in a narrow place. Another car comes up behind, containing the gunmen for the snatch; or they may emerge from the crowd on the pavement or from the blocking van. A variant, used on a more open road, is for the terrorists to be dressed as policemen doing a road check. If the victim has an escort car there may be a separate team to deal with this. The victim is then driven away either in his own car or in the kidnappers' car or van. He will almost certainly be transferred to another vehicle within a few miles. There may—as described above for Geoffrey Jackson's kidnap—be other teams to block access roads, and other observers to report the presence or absence of police cars on the exit route. The head of the snatch squad will have alternative plans in case the exit route or the transfer spot to the new vehicle are reported to be unsafe.

2. Geoffrey Jackson, *op cit.*

Many variations are possible. If the victim has to walk from his front door to an outside garage, or get out of his car to open the garage on his return, this may be the easiest snatch point. One industrialist in Italy regularly crossed the street outside his factory to a particular restaurant for lunch; another was in the habit of working late and leaving by a side gate which led into a quiet street. In both cases the kidnappers did not need to bother about the precise time, and a single car was all they needed for the snatch of a victim who was on foot.

Kidnappings at the victim's home are more difficult (except immediately outside it, as described), and usually involve entry by subterfuge: to read the meter, or to deliver a gift. This is unlikely to be attempted if the victim is prepared for the threat and takes proper precautions (see pages 96-8)—though treachery can breach the strongest defences (as in the case of Jürgen Ponto—see page 38). Kidnapping from inside the office is more difficult still, unless entry and exit are wholly unrestricted, but may be attractive if there is scope for staff infiltration or treachery.

Regular habits of any kind may offer opportunities to kidnappers. One US air attaché in the Dominican Republic for example, was always to be found (and was picked up) at 6 a.m. doing callisthenics on a polo field.

Kidnappers will also take advantage of any opportunity which will delay notification that the victim is missing—as, for example, in the case quoted in Chapter Sixteen. Here, they picked an evening when his family was away and he was going to have a workout in a gymnasium on his way home; the gym attached no significance to his not coming, while he was not expected at home for three hours—valuable hours for the kidnappers.

HOLDING AND INTERROGATION OF A HOSTAGE

Hostages are most often held in urban areas, though isolated farmhouses have been used. The typical hideout is in a small suburban house or flat. The 'prison' may be in a concealed cellar, which is less vulnerable to police search; or it may be in a normal room, in which case the victim is likely to be permanently blind-

folded lest he remembers details of wallpaper, or the view from a
window, which might later be useful to the police. Some victims
have been held in tents erected inside a large living room, for this
same reason.

Guarding the prisoner is often a task for low-grade and ex-
pendable members of the gang, because they are the likeliest to
be caught, either in a police raid or because a released victim may
be able to identify them later by their voices or (even though they
are hooded) by their eyes. The organizers will therefore wish
them to be in possession of as little information as possible. They
may sometimes be small-time criminals or students, hired for the
job without being told anything about the organization behind it.

Sometimes higher members of the gang may visit the hostage
to question him or to discuss points which have arisen in negotiation. In political kidnappings this interrogation may be an important part of the operation, and the interrogator may use physical torture; but this arouses hatred and in the end strengthens
resistance. More subtle and effective are the techniques of mental disorientation: e.g. by humiliation and degradation; by denial
of sleep and food; by continual blindfolding and earplugging, or
by periods of noise and light alternated with total silence and
darkness. In such cases the interrogator is likely to hold a responsible position in the group, and may well stay for a long time with
the hostage in order to build up a relationship of psychological
dependance (by total reliance on his captor for food, comfort and
human contact). Such dependance has on many occasions developed into rapport, which can operate in both directions. This is
discussed further in Chapter Eight.

PUBLICITY AND PROPAGANDA

In political kidnappings, publicity may be a primary aim; and
there may be demands for the broadcasting of manifestos or the
distribution of food to the poor, as well as for the release of
prisoners and payment of ransom. Photographs of several victims
(e.g. Peter Lorenz and Hanns-Martin Schleyer) were issued to
the press with a notice reading 'Prisoner of the Red Army
Fraction' as a background to give status to the movement. The

same technique was used by the Red Brigades with Aldo Moro. Dr Schleyer was made to give a filmed interview which appeared on television worldwide before they killed him. Visits by selected journalists may be arranged.

On the other hand, the political connection may be concealed in order to avoid government intervention—at least until the ransom has been paid. Purely criminal kidnappers will usually try to avoid publicity altogether, in the hope that the victim's family may settle without the police or the public ever knowing that he was kidnapped.

NEGOTIATION

The first kidnap telephone call or written message will invariably include a dire warning not to inform the police. It will also aim to establish psychological domination for the kidnappers from the start. In a well planned kidnap, this may be a major factor in the choice of who is first to be informed.

The kidnappers will also demand an immediate settlement, while the victim's family or colleagues are in a state of shock, and before they realize that the victim is unlikely to be killed in a hurry if the aim is to exchange him for money—though the kidnappers will of course threaten to do so.

If the kidnappers have done their homework, they will have an idea of how much the victim's family or firm can pay. They will usually demand much more than this to leave room for negotiation (a settlement of a fifth of the original demand has been fairly common). They may, however, pick a sum which could conceivably be raised in the hope of bouncing an immediate settlement. In either case, their reaction to the inevitable reply of inability to meet the first demand will usually be harsh and peremptory: 'If you want to see him alive you'd better agree to pay right away. We are not interested in haggling. Unless you agree by ten o'clock we will kill him.'

If the family or firm do not panic, the kidnappers may resign themselves to a long haul, and their main anxiety will be to keep the police out of the negotiations and to frighten the negotiators into negotiating on a telephone that is not tapped. An example of this is given in Chapter Sixteen. They will also probably agree to the establishment of continuity of negotiators on both sides, so that they know each other's voices (or use an agreed codeword). This guards against some rival criminal gang making spurious arrangements for the handover of a ransom.

The techniques of coercive bargaining are further discussed in Chapters Nine and Ten.

COLLECTING THE MONEY AND RELEASING THE VICTIM

Whatever other demands the terrorists may make (e.g. by way of political blackmail or propaganda) it is when they are collecting a ransom that they are most vulnerable.

They are very unlikely to agree to the simultaneous exchange of the money and the victim, for many obvious reasons—unless they are worried that the police are closing in on them, and feel that it is worth the risk of settling quickly by an exchange if that is all that the family or firm will accept. A major anxiety is to ensure that the money cannot be traced. They are likely to demand notes of small denomination, not with consecutive numbers.

Their greatest concern, however, is to ensure that the handover is not ambushed, or observed by the police. They are aware that, even if they have frightened the negotiators into keeping the police in the dark, the police may have tapped the telephone without the negotiators knowing. They normally, therefore, insist on a series of 'treasure-hunt' clues in a complicated plan to drop the money, each of which can be watched to ensure that the person dropping it is not being followed.

A typical arrangement would be that the dropper must go, with the money in a suitcase, to (say) a public lavatory to pick up the first clue. This might instruct him to go to a certain spot to pick up an abandoned car and drive it on a stated route at a stated speed to a third point, where he is to leave the car and walk away down a long street—with a warning that if he turns round he will immediately be shot. Only when he is clear will the kidnappers emerge to drive away the car; and they in turn will probably switch very quickly to another car in a deserted place before the dropper (who might well be a police 'plant') has had time to report a description of the first one.

The terrorists will want first to rule out any risk of ambush, and second to avoid being seen by monitoring police at a range close enough for identification; and they will want to be sure that they have shaken off any monitors before they risk being seen at close quarters by anyone at all.

Some gangs may attempt to break faith and kill the victim after receiving and proving the money, because they fear that he could give them away, or because they intended to murder him in the first place, for political reasons, or for revenge or as a deterrent. Other groups may attempt to get a second or even a third ransom for the same hostage. This has been done in several cases, but (because the drop gives the police the best chance of establishing a lead) it greatly increases the gang's vulnerability thereafter. That is why it is not tried more often.

DISPERSAL OF THE MONEY

One of the commonest leads into a criminal gang comes when one or more of its members is seen to have a lot of money to spend. Kidnappers will therefore be cautious about this. International organizations (criminal or political) will probably try to get the money out of the country as soon as they can, probably into bank accounts in the names of people who have no discernible link with them. In Europe, the ease of movement within the EEC facilitates this. Large criminal groups like the Mafia, if they do not get the money across a frontier, will at least try to mount operations far from their base; e.g. they will obtain the money in Milan and spend it in Calabria or Sicily.

Otherwise, they may recycle the money, first ensuring that it is genuine, and then converting it in small amounts at a time into goods or other money, watching carefully to detect any reaction. They may not release their hostage until they have done all this.

TERRORIST STRENGTHS AND WEAKNESSES

The normal reactions of the family or colleagues on hearing

c

that the victim has been kidnapped are panic and despair.
The terrorists seem to hold all the cards, but in fact they do
not.

The cost of mounting a kidnapping operation may be very
high. It has been estimated that in Italy a target study of the
victim and the reconnaisance costs about $30,000; members of
the snatch group are likely to be paid $10,000 to $15,000 each—
that is, about $60,000 in all; guards are paid $2,000 a month,
plus a percentage of the final ransom as a bonus; finally, the
recycling of the money will probably cost 30–40 per cent of the
ransom. Thus, for a million-dollar ransom, the overheads for an
average gang will be about $250,000 out of the $600,000 to
$700,000 total of recycled money received.

A further weakness is that, since the amounts received by the
rank and file are comparatively small in relation to the high risk,
the offer of a generous reward for the recovery of the victim may
be very attractive to them.

The terrorists do, however, have certain enormous advantages.
First, they have the initiative: they have a plan from which,
unless they are amateurs, they can visualize developments at
each stage, with alternatives to meet the unexpected. Second,
they hold the victim, and they know where everyone on both
sides is based, so they can watch and monitor while the police
and negotiators initially cannot. Third, the kidnappers are willing to kill or maim their victim, while the authorities (in most
countries) recognize self-imposed restraints; the British police,
for example, are proud of the fact that while terrorists in England
killed sixty-four people (including two policemen) between 1973
and 1977, they arrested 148 of them without killing or injuring a
single one.

A fourth advantage is that the terrorists know that most people
will pay rather than allow a husband or child or colleague to be
killed; and that the majority of kidnappings do succeed—at least
in the short term. In Italy since 1970 there have been about 500
reported kidnappings, though the actual number may be many
more. Six of the victims are known to be dead, and another
twenty-eight presumed so. About $80 million was paid in ran-
soms in the reported cases—and the average takings were many
times greater than in bank robberies, with less risk. Only about

10 per cent of the kidnappers have been arrested and 5 per cent convicted.

The terrorists, however, are well aware of their own weaknesses, and they face the constant tension of the hunted animal. They know that if they kill their hostage before they have received and proved their ransom, they are unlikely to get a ransom at all, since the negotiators will demand up-to-date proof that the victim is alive before they pay. Moreover, once the police suspect that the hostage is dead, they will have no inhibitions about shooting to kill if they do run the gang to earth. For those reasons they know that in killing their hostage they are playing their last card, which can then be trumped as soon as it is recognized; and they realize that the victim, the negotiators and the police all know that this is so.

The kidnappers' greatest weakness is that time is on the side of the police, whether measured in days or months. Every extra day brings greater chance of detection, and may accumulate more evidence for eventual arrest and conviction. Every tapped telephone call increases the risk, and increases the pressure on the kidnapper to settle for what he can get before he loses all.

II. THE RESPONSE

Chapter Five

Response in a Pluralist Society

TOTALITARIAN, AUTHORITARIAN AND DEMOCRATIC STATES

THE security director of an American firm which markets world-wide once told the author that the countries in which he had the least problems in protecting staff and assets were behind the iron curtain, but that he would hate to live there. Sir Robert Mark, ex-commissioner of the Metropolitan Police, has said: 'Total freedom is anarchy; total order is tyranny.'

Truly democratic societies are, of course, particularly vulnerable to individuals who are prepared to kill to further their aims, but who expect to enjoy the protection of civil rights and laws which rely upon a voluntary respect by the community for the rule of law. Their governments are properly reluctant to discriminate between citizens before they commit a crime, or to curtail the freedom of millions to protect them against the violence of a few. Though citizens of such societies may have to suffer grievously for retaining their freedoms (as in Germany), they are in the long run the best able to resist terrorism.

Terrorism thrives most in societies in which the democratic system is weak or corrupt, or which fall between the two extremes: that is, those which are authoritarian rather than either totalitarian or truly democratic. Thus Italy, of all West European countries, suffers most, because the democratic process enjoys little confidence and the administration is weak. But terrorism has been worst of all in a number of Latin-American countries, where government is oppressive enough to arouse substantial numbers of people to use or support violence to resist it, while the administration and law-enforcement agencies are corrupt or are not efficient enough to contain this violence. Once violence is seen to pay—in political or financial dividends—and is seen to carry little risk of punishment, it will grow. If societies like this do eventually contain terrorism, it is more likely to be by moving towards totalitarianism than towards democracy.

Totalitarian societies are outside the scope of this book; there are only about a score of them in the world, all claiming to be communist, but mostly much closer to the fascism of Hitler and Stalin. The book does apply to all the other kinds of society in which readers are likely to find themselves living or working: these include authoritarian states and democratic states, ranging in both types from those which are efficiently run to those which are chaotic, inequitable or corrupt. All of these can be defined as pluralist, in that they do not live under a single all-powerful authority controlling all others, but under a balance of some or all of a number of conflicting forces, such as political parties, governments, bureaucracies, armies, police forces, judiciaries, industries, trade unions, banks, mass media and pressure groups —and in some cases powerful illegal or criminal organizations. An individual, family or corporation seeking for self-protection against violence or coercion in such societies has to take account of all of these forces, and to find a way of working together with those which can help him.

CONFLICTING INTERESTS

The problem is that the interests of those involved on the side of the law will often conflict.

The victim has interests that conflict in themselves: as a potential victim, merely assessing the risk of kidnap, he has to balance cost and inconvenience against the degree of risk and security; he may prefer to take a risk rather than prejudice the efficiency of his work or sacrifice the pleasures and varieties of his life; or he may be reluctant to seem scared or to place a burden on his firm or his family.

Once kidnapped, he will of course place a far greater burden on them. He will be fighting for survival, but he will probably prefer to die than to do certain things, such as betraying his wife or children or a close colleague. Some victims will choose to die rather than connive at the paying of a ransom or the release of imprisoned terrorists who will go on to kill others.

His family will probably be less willing to sacrifice his life than he is himself. If the victim is a small child, they will not sacrifice it under any circumstances. The family will probably be wise not to try to negotiate for themselves, because emotion would play too big a part, but they will be able to give indispensable information and support to those negotiating for them.

His negotiators—and *lawyers* of the family or the firm, who are frequently themselves the negotiators—have a duty to balance their obligations to their client and their obligations, legal or moral, as citizens. They carry an enormous strain, and must avoid becoming too emotionally involved. They need all the support and freedom of action they can be given.

His firm may well be involved in that the victim is kidnapped to extort money from it. The firm, too, has to balance its responsibility to the victim against its responsibility to its other employees and to its stockholders. It may have a legal responsibility for adequate protection of its personnel: at least one kidnap victim is known to have sued his firm. It has also to guard its reputation and the morale of its staff. It may face a conflict between these obligations and observance of the laws.

Corporate headquarters—if the firm is a subsidiary of an overseas corporation—may see the problem differently from its representatives on the ground. The corporation has financial responsibility; and has to consider not only morale, but the potential threat to its other subsidiaries if it gives way too easily. A communication problem may arise at vital moments of decision during negotiation.

The police have a dual responsibility: to the victim and to society.

The army may, in some countries, act instead of the police in terrorist operations; or the two may to some extent be rivals.

Neither will wish to tarnish its reputation for firmness or efficiency. On the other hand, they will be unwise to be seen as manifestly unfeeling, or to forfeit the co-operation of the victim's family or firm. Their primary aim will be detection, arrest and conviction; and for this such co-operation is vital. It is also most important to handle the case in such a way as not to deter such co-operation in further cases.

Security firms and advisers are often involved. Firms, usually routinely engaged by companies, are responsible to those who engaged them, subject to the law. It is essential that they work in co-operation with the police, not in competition; and the police should recognize their legitimacy and their value as allies. Most companies employ security firms, at least for the installation of burglar alarms, if not for guards.

The firm or family may also engage a security adviser especially to deal with the incident. When a kidnapping occurs, the victim's family or colleagues are usually taken wholly by surprise. They have seldom any previous experience of negotiating for someone's life; nor, as a rule, do their lawyers or other negotiators. They therefore risk acting unwisely: e.g. by paying an unduly high ransom, or paying too quickly. An experienced adviser will have handled such situations before. His advice is likely to assist the negotiator in reducing the ransom, and in protracting the negotiations. Terrorists are reluctant to play the final card of killing their victim, for this ends their chance of a ransom. They do have weak points as described in the previous chapter; and the longer their own ordeal, the more they will feel the strain. Professionally advised negotiation can greatly increase the time available for the police for detection and arrest, and help them in gaining evidence to convict.

The judiciary and the legislature may both be involved in serious cases, and are in any case concerned with the provisions and operation of the laws under which the battle (and future battles) will be fought. If these laws are unrealistic, people will bypass them. If, for example, the payment of ransoms is illegal, a distraught family will keep the police in the dark rather than allow the victim to be murdered, especially if it is a small child. And punishing people who act under duress can only do harm to future respect by the community for the law.

The mass media will not forgo sensational news unless they are confident that all their rivals will also forgo it. This has sometimes been achieved when the public is unaware of the kidnapping. For example, in London in 1975, a Cypriot girl was kidnapped (see Chapter Eleven). The family told the police and no one else; but the kidnappers were unaware that the police had been informed. The commissioner of police briefed all editors together, telling them that the girl's life would be at stake if any of them broke his plea for silence. They all respected the plea, and ten days later the girl was rescued and all the kidnappers arrested.

It is, however, rare for a case to be so insulated as this one. In authoritarian countries, the media may be state-controlled or censored. Where there is a free press, the story cannot be stifled once it has leaked out; so the only sensible reaction is to live with the media, and try to understand and predict the line they will take. It is possible to reward co-operative journalists with better access and information, and to punish others by withholding it. Editors will pay dearly in the long run if their irresponsibility causes unnecessary suffering or loss of life.

The government stands over all these agencies and individuals. It will want to retain its credibility and reputation for firmness; but it will not want to appear unfeeling, nor to forfeit public support and co-operation by doing so. If the case appears to be a purely criminal one, it will probably try to keep out of it. If the kidnapping poses a political challenge, the government may have no alternative but to sacrifice the victim rather than to give way.

Overseas governments may also be involved if the victim or his firm are expatriates. They will be concerned over the relationship with the host country, and the prospects for their commercial activities in it; they will also wish to maintain their image in the world, and to discourage further attacks upon their nationals; but they may be even more concerned about their standing inside their own countries.

SECURITY PRECAUTIONS AND CONTINGENCY PLANNING

Planning to prevent or handle terrorist attack is, for the kind of people likely to be selected as victims, at least as important as taking precautions against fire or burglary.

It must begin with analysis: assessing the threat both of the likelihood and of the form of attack; and what the price of failure to deter or defeat such an attack might be in terms of lives, staff morale, money or disruption. The next decision (as with protection against fire or burglary) is how much it is worth spending—again in terms of money and inconvenience—to prevent it or to minimize its effects. This leads to action: first in the form of security measures and physical protection; and second in the form of contingency planning for crisis management. These protective and security measures and contingency plans need to be constantly reviewed in the light of a varying threat. They should therefore contain provision for a sudden increase in the degree of alertness and security—just as an army defending a frontier has different states of readiness and deployment.

An important function of contingency planning is to ensure that those who may suddenly be faced with a crisis have thought how they would respond. Families have a natural reluctance to face the possibility that one of them may be kidnapped. So do business firms and in their case their chief executive may himself be the victim at the precise moment when the plan has to be put into effect.

A co-ordinated response is vitally important—particularly the initial response to a kidnap message, which is likely to set the tone for subsequent negotiations. The kidnappers themselves will be in a state of acute tension; and a cool, determined response by people who give the impression that they know what they are doing and will be hard to crack may have a decisive psychological effect.

A co-ordinated response necessitates prior discussion and co-operation between the various agencies listed earlier in this chapter and this will be examined in more detail in later chapters. The initiative will normally have to be taken by the potential victims or firms which see themselves as under threat, and they may find it worthwhile to seek to create trust and confidence between themselves and the agencies. In a country where corruption or treachery are suspected this may be very difficult, and may in extreme cases make it inadvisable to live and work in that country at all. This, of course, is often the primary aim of political terrorist movements; and they will therefore do their best to spread corruption amongst police and officials—which has the added effect of alienating public support for the government. All that expatriates—whether representing their governments or multinational corporations—can do in those circumstances is to give warning of the risk of losing foreign investment and trade, as well as the loss of internal stability; and try to provide some incentive for the creation of a climate in which co-operation for security becomes possible.

Chapter Six

The Government, The Police and The Law

INTERNATIONAL CO-OPERATION

IF all governments were perfect, with prosperous and egalitarian societies, fair but effective laws, wholly uncorrupt administration and police forces, a free but responsible press and no foreign interference, it can be argued that there would be no need for terrorism, or even demonstrations of dissent. Paradoxically, however, the experience of West Germany suggests that popular contentment with government may so frustrate the revolutionaries that they turn to violence (see Chapter Two). Be that as it may, it is clearly the first duty of a democratic government to work towards these things; but that is outside the scope of this book, which must deal with societies as they are: authoritarian or democratic, efficient or chaotic, honest or corrupt, but never perfect.

So, these perfections aside, a government's first responsibility is to encourage international co-operation against terrorism, above all by itself setting a good example of such co-operation. One element of this is to refuse to treat terrorism as a political crime, whose perpetrators are immune from extradition; another is to exchange intelligence information, which is best done on a bilateral basis rather than through international agencies such as Interpol. An important factor in reducing hijacking of aircraft in the USA was a bilateral agreement between the USA and Cuba. More recently, in 1978, the USA introduced legislation to impose sanctions (such as the withdrawal of air transport facilities in both directions) against countries which have inadequate airport search standards, or which harbour terrorists. Such sanctions were initially discretionary, on a case by case basis; but even these, from a powerful country like the USA, could be very effective. They could become decisive if all countries did the same—though there is as yet sadly little prospect of this. One weapon which should be exploited to the full is the fuelling of world revulsion against terrorism by publicizing the sufferings of innocent victims and of their families.

CO-ORDINATION OF SECURITY AND RESPONSE

A primary responsibility of a government inside its own country is to encourage and co-ordinate both security precautions against terrorism and the response to it if it occurs. In theory the authoritarian state might seem able to do this better; but in practice a democratic state is more effective, in that it can co-ordinate the voluntary efforts of many different brains rather than rely on people carrying out the instructions of a small pyramid of predictably conformist brains at the top. This probably accounts for the remarkable record of arrest and conviction of kidnappers in the USA (see page 20) and the very low incidence of kidnapping in Great Britain.

The US government has led the way by establishing a section in the State Department to combat terrorism, and a Special Co-ordinating Committee (SCC) of the National Security Council, to convene immediately in the event of a major terrorist incident to handle crisis management. In Britain, the Home Secretary is charged with convening an equivalent body, and Scotland Yard has an operations centre in readiness to co-ordinate the response.

These arrangements are primarily to deal with terrorist acts with a political aim; but where criminal kidnappings are rife, something at a lower level is required.

In Italy, where reported kidnappings average six per month, an examining magistrate is appointed to co-ordinate the response in each case. This can be an asset, but it may be a liability if he imposes restrictions on negotiations which drive the family in desperation to act independently of the police. This is further discussed later in the chapter.

The art of democratic government is to understand and harness the motivations of those involved; to recognize that though their priorities may differ, they do all share the two aims of saving the life of the victim and arresting his kidnappers; and so to stage-manage the response as to give full rein to the dynamism created by these motivations to achieve both of these aims.

This applies to preventive measures as well as to crisis management. Commercial firms and individuals who are vulnerable should be encouraged to adopt effective security precautions, and to establish liaison with the police, which should also be extended to any security firms and advisers whom they employ. Assistance should be given where possible, e.g. in providing alternative or direct means of communication.

LAWS AGAINST TERRORISM

Laws which inhibit the operation or the support of terrorists are to be encouraged; while those which inhibit the freedom of action of negotiators are generally counterproductive.

The first essential for controlling terrorism is a system of effective laws covering firearms and explosives. In some countries, these laws are so bad that they lead to a vicious circle, in which ever widening possession of firearms by criminals is taken to justify wider possession by others, making it easier still for criminals to get them. This is so in the USA, where the homicide and bombing rates (though not the kidnapping rate) are amongst the highest in the world.

The second essential is for the law to facilitate detection, arrest *and conviction* of terrorists. The likelihood of arrest and conviction is a far greater deterrent than the scale of punishment, even if that punishment includes the death penalty. In framing these laws, however, a delicate balance must be struck. If they are too repressive, they may increase the very small percentage of the population which is prepared to give active support and shelter to terrorists, and alienate a larger percentage who may be driven to feel some sympathy for those who can claim to be fighting the repression. On the other hand, if the laws are ineffective, an exasperated public may take the law into its own hands (with vigilante groups and assassination squads), and a frustrated police force may be tempted to connive at the murder of members of one gang by another; both of these things spell the virtual certainty of a democratic society lapsing into authoritarianism of the right or left, or even into totalitarianism.

After the killing of twenty-one people by the IRA in two pub bombings in Birmingham, the British government introduced the Prevention of Terrorism (Temporary Provisions) Act of 1974, which was renewed each year thereafter. Among other provisions, this act increased the time for which a person could be held under arrest prior to being charged from two days to seven (subject to Home Office approval in each individual case). On the other hand, the government resisted public pressure to change the rules governing police interrogation and confessions, or to reintroduce the death penalty. The balance of the act was probably about right, and it proved effective.

In February 1978 the West German government, following the 1977 murders and kidnappings by the Red Army Fraction, also introduced anti-terrorist legislation which permitted the police to set up road checks; to search whole blocks rather than just individual flats; to hold for twelve hours anyone who could not satisfactorily establish his identity (even if not specifically suspected of a crime); to exclude lawyers from appearing in court if there were sufficient grounds for suspicion that they themselves had been involved in supporting terrorism; and to permit the insertion of a glass barrier between a prisoner and his lawyer during interviews in gaol. This last was to counter the proven practice of lawyers exchanging messages and smuggling weapons, explosives and radios to convicted Red Army Fraction terrorists in Stammheim Prison. Again the public (and the Parliamentary Opposition) demanded much more, including monitoring of conversations between prisoners and their lawyers, and the preventive custody of convicted terrorists after completion of their sentences. Chancellor Schmidt's government, however, was very sensitive to accusations of recrudescent Nazism, and was reluctant to take measures which might increase the number of those who sympathized with the terrorists (see pages 36 and 37). As it was, the measures were passed by only one vote, the Christian Democrats opposing them because they were too weak, and a handful of left-wing Social Democrats because they were too repressive.

In March 1978, after the kidnapping of Aldo Moro, the Italian parliament (including the Communist Party) overwhelmingly supported government measures to give the police greater powers for holding and interrogating suspects—including the power to interrogate them without their lawyers being present—and greater powers of search, tapping of telephones, etc.

LAWS AFFECTING NEGOTIATIONS

Some countries have attempted to make laws which are not aimed directly at the terrorists, but to inhibit certain actions by those negotiating for the victim's release. These include the freezing of assets; banning of the payment of ransoms; banning of insurance indemnity against ransoms; and even trying to bar communication with the kidnappers altogether. Such laws are in practice almost wholly counterproductive.

This may at first seem surprising. In the case of the kidnapping of diplomats, the firm refusal of some governments to pay ransoms or release prisoners, no matter what the cost to the victim, has been the most effective of all deterrents. The US government again led the way in this respect. Between 1968 and 1974, twenty-seven US officials with diplomatic status were kidnapped. The US government resolutely refused to pay ransoms, or to make any concessions whatever to political blackmail; and declared that in no circumstances would they do so. As a direct result of this hard line, ten of the twenty-seven were killed and twelve wounded—an appalling casualty rate. Yet every US diplomat with whom the author has discussed this supported the policy, on the grounds that if ever the US government had given way, the numbers kidnapped would have soared into hundreds, and the number killed would have been far more than ten. A diplomat accepts that he may have to die rather than sacrifice his country's interests—just as a soldier would not expect his army to abandon a vital position just because his life was in danger. It was with this in mind that Geoffrey Jackson and his wife, who perceived that he was about to be a target for kidnapping by the Tupamaros, told the British Foreign Office in advance that they wished no concessions to be made to the kidnappers, nor any pressure to be put on the Uruguayan government to do so.

The Israeli government, with evident support from its people, has also consistently refused to give way; even when ninety school-children were held by Palestinian terrorists at Ma'alot in 1974, they held firm, with the result that twenty of the children were killed. Again the Israeli people were convinced that, if they had given way, the number of terrorist raids and the number killed in them would have been increased; indeed, they felt that the very existence of their country was at stake. And both the German people and the world applauded Helmut Schmidt's courageous decision in October 1977 to accept the death of Hanns-Martin Schleyer rather than release other terrorists or to give in to the demands of the hijackers at Mogadishu.

If it was right for the US, Israeli and German governments to stand firm, why is it counterproductive for governments to forbid the payment of ransoms by private individuals or corporations? The answer lies in the fact that the demand was in all cases for the release of other terrorists who would, as experience has proved, be likely thereafter to kill other people.

When the demand is made to a family or corporation, it is almost invariably for a ransom; they have no power to release prisoners nor (except in marginal ways concerned with propaganda) to provide anything that the kidnappers might want other than money. While it can be argued that it is wrong to pay money to criminal gangs which may thereby be encouraged and helped to commit more crimes, it is unlikely that the victim's family or colleagues will think that this matters more than his life. Nor is there any evidence that a family or firm which once pays a ransom is likelier to be picked as a target again; on the contrary, having been bitten, they almost always so intensify their security precautions that kidnappers prefer to turn to a softer target.

For both human and commercial reasons, they will usually pay rather than let him die. If there are laws to inhibit the payment of a ransom, they will, with a life at stake, justify finding a way round them, and in so doing will reduce the chances of arrest and conviction of the kidnappers.

This was well brought out in the consideration of three bills brought before the Californian State Senate after the kidnapping of Patty Hearst in 1974. These bills sought to outlaw the payment of ransoms either from the assets of a charitable trust or from corporate assets. Trustees or corporate officials who made or approved such payments would become personally liable for the full amount paid.

Brian Jenkins, who was at that time researching terrorism for the Rand Corporation, was asked for written comments before the bills were discussed, and these were published.[1] He argued most convincingly against the bills. He considered first that they would not deter the kidnappers, who cared not at all whether the man paying the ransom was breaking the law; second that the victim's family or firm would not be deterred from paying if they believed that his life was at stake; third that, since they would be forced to keep the payment secret from the police, the prospects of detection and arrest of the criminals would be greatly reduced, and that the greatest deterrent of all—conviction—would thereby be made less likely.

For these and other reasons the bills were defeated.

Equally convincing arguments can be applied to almost any legislation which restricts freedom of action of those negotiating for the release of a hostage. At first sight, for example, it might appear that insurance indemnity against ransom payments would make the victim more ready to pay more money more quickly, and less ready to co-operate with the police. In practice the reverse is the case. There is no doubt that the existence of insurance cover has reduced the chances of a person being selected as a kidnap victim, has reduced the amount paid in ransoms, has extended the duration of negotiations, and has thereby increased the chance of arrest of the kidnappers. The reasons for this are discussed in the next chapter.

The fact remains that commercial firms will in any event find ways of paying ransoms rather than let their executives die, because they know that they could not get top-rate executives to work in high-risk areas if they did not, and that the adverse effect on staff morale would cost more than the ransom. Sophisti-

1. Brian Jenkins, *Should Corporations be Prevented from Paying Ransom?* (Rand Corporation, Santa Monica, 1974).

cated kidnappers are well aware of this. The wife of a kidnapped husband or the father of a kidnapped child is still less likely to be deterred from saving his life by the threat of prosecution; nor is public opinion likely to tolerate their conviction if they do.

The twin aims of saving the hostage's life and arresting the kidnappers must and can be harnessed together. If firms or families are driven by fear of prosecution to act independently, they will almost certainly pay a much larger ransom (which gives more power to the terrorists), and do so much more quickly (which reduces the chance of detection). Both of these things are contrary to the interests of the government and of the police. If, on the other hand, the negotiators know that they can be frank with the police, they will welcome police co-operation. The police, for their part, can only get the information they need to achieve detection—and the time to do so—by co-operation with the negotiators.

THE POLICE AND THE NEGOTIATORS

The information and assistance which the police can get from the negotiators includes a description of the victim, of the clothes he was wearing, his state of health, and his likely reactions to incarceration and (if discovered) to a raid to rescue him. The negotiators can be asked to speak only from tapped telephones, to log and report all communications (telephone or otherwise) and to tell the police the details of any plan for dropping the money or picking up the victim. The negotiators are the only people who can provide the means of positive proof that the victim is still alive (e.g. by identifying his voice or handwriting, or by suggesting personal questions which only he could answer). Above all, the police can advise the negotiators on how best to protract the negotiations, and how best to handle them so that the kidnappers can be arrested, either before or after collecting the ransom. The police will achieve none of these things unless they recognize—and are seen to recognize—that the primary motivation of the negotiators is to save the victim's life. They will do best if they make use of the power of this motivation rather than try to frustrate it. The best chance of detection is at or after the drop, and for this the co-operation of the negotiators is almost indispensable.

POLICE ORGANIZATION, TRAINING AND EQUIPMENT

Policemen must be well paid; otherwise it can be taken as certain that a sophisticated kidnapping team, with huge sums of money at stake, will be able to corrupt at least one key man in the organization. (It must in any case be regarded as certain that they will *try* to do so.)

When the crunch comes, a policeman—like a soldier—must be ready to risk his life to save the victim or to arrest the kidnappers. This demands a level of morale and dedication which can only be achieved by intensive training, good equipment, good personnel management, and confidence that his family will be looked after. Experience has proved over and over again that soldiers, bodyguards and policemen *can* be motivated to this degree of self-sacrifice; and police forces must master the training skills— and receive the government backing—for doing so.

The first essential for the policeman is confidence in his weapons, and training in using them in close-quarters fighting.

Training in acquiring and collating intelligence is equally important, if less spectacular. This will require adequate funds for paying rewards, coupled with an effective system to prevent fraud and embezzlement of these funds. Intelligence gathering also requires skills in the use of transducers, voice identification, graphology, bugging (and counterbugging) and covert cameras.

PUBLIC RELATIONS

The government and the police must have a shrewd understanding of the press, radio and television. Like negotiators, journalists have predictable motivations. If they are asked for co-operation or restraint they will expect not only to be treated fairly in relation to their rivals, but also to be rewarded later with access to news when it is available. They will also be aware that if they do not co-operate they will have no hope of such rewards on any future occasion.

Kidnapping, like all forms of terrorism, gives the police un-rivalled opportunities for improving their image. The over-whelming majority of the public detests kidnappers, and will applaud the police if they are caught. Provided that they feel reasonable confidence in police protection and discretion, most people will be willing to help with information, and if necessary give active co-operation against kidnappers. If the police co-operate with the media in getting the news sympathetically presented—including the more loathesome aspects of the kid-napping, detention and maltreatment of a hostage, and the ago-nies of his family—it will be wholly to their advantage. If they are seen to sympathize with the feelings of the family, and not to be driving heartlessly for an arrest without regard to these feelings, each kidnapping should substantially increase the co-operation of the public, both in combating terrorism, and as regards police activities in general.

Chapter Seven

Security Precautions by Management and Individuals

MINIMIZING FINANCIAL AND HUMAN DAMAGE

A corporation's duty is first to its employees and their families, and then to its stockholders. The kidnapping of a member of the firm can do immense financial and human damage but if the firm does not give the prevention of human damage the higher priority, it is likely to lose more financially in the long run. A corporation which fails to take care of its own people may pay very heavily. It will acquire an unflattering public image, face a disastrous decline in staff morale, and be unable to attract capable staff to work in high-risk areas, or even to maintain its operations in these areas at all.

This—the abandonment of capital development—may, of course, be the primary aim of political terrorists, especially in Latin America. That makes it all the more incumbent on corporations to protect their staff, and to convince the government and public of the cost to themselves, in terms of unemployment and revenue, of the cessation of the corporation's activity.

ASSESSING AND REDUCING THE RISK

The first step is to make a realistic assessment of the risk. The easiest course is always to push it under the carpet and do nothing—on the grounds that 'it won't happen to us', or that 'if they are after us nothing will stop them', or that 'we cannot operate efficiently if we tie our hands with security precautions.'

The greatest single factor in reducing the risk is to be seen to take active security precautions. Neither political terrorists nor criminals can afford a fiasco, so they always look for a soft target. The more evident the security precautions, the more likely they are to turn away: 'there is always another mug.'

The approach should be the same as in assessing and guarding against the risk of fire and theft. The better the precautions, the less the risk of it happening at all. But if it does happen, what will be the cost of the damage, and how can it be reduced? How much, therefore, is the firm prepared to spend on, for example, locks, burglar alarms, fire doors, sprinklers and insurance? A wise man will call in a fire surveyor—indeed, his insurance company may insist upon him doing so, or send one themselves. On the same reasoning, a wise firm will call for a security survey, or seek guidance from the police crime prevention officer.

Reducing fire risks requires both fire prevention and plans and equipment to fight the fire. Similarly, reducing the risks of kidnapping—both of its occurrence and of its cost—requires preventive measures and contingency planning for crisis management.

The Potential Target

Kidnap security consists of security of individuals or of members of their families, whether the extortion is to be from their private wealth or from corporate assets. The individual is vulnerable at work, and (with his family) at home or on the road.

The greatest enemy to security is again usually the individual's desire to push the matter under the carpet—the attitude that 'it won't happen', or 'if they want me they'll get me', or 'I can't do my job if I hem myself in', or 'I'd rather take the risk than live a life that is not worth living.' An executive who is a likely target should obviously maintain a low profile and take care that his movements are not predictable; yet he may feel that the prestige of his firm requires him to take an active part in public functions —as many other public figures have to do.

The solution lies in a reasonable balance, taking account of the intensity of the risk and the problems of guarding against it. A 100 per cent security against kidnapping is no more possible than a 100 per cent security against fire or theft; but, as with a firm so with an individual, the kidnapper will usually look elsewhere if security is manifestly good. There will be exceptions to this (as with Hanns-Martin Schleyer or Aldo Moro); and in those cases much will depend on the participation and efficiency of government law-enforcement agencies.

Protection is never impossible. King Hussein, who saw his grandfather assassinated, has survived a quarter of a century of constant threat without at any time withdrawing from public life. General de Gaulle never shirked his public responsibilities and he survived thirty-one attempts on his life. Obviously they depended upon a major deployment of security resources, but many Chinese millionaires and their families in South and East Asia have lived all their lives under some kind of protection from kidnapping. The cost of being kidnapped will be many times greater than the cost of preventing it.

Co-operation with Government and Police

Most governments will wish to co-operate in protecting likely victims, since kidnapping does serious damage both to their prestige and to the confidence of the international community in investing and trading with their country.

Firms and individuals who are targets should establish contact with government officials and police (and other security forces, such as the army, where appropriate) at the highest possible level. If they are expatriates, it may be wise to involve their embassy or consular officials.

The most serious problems arise if there is suspicion that government officials or police officers may be corrupt or treacherous. If key officials or police officers are in league with a criminal or political terrorist group, it may make little difference whether the firm or individual has contacts or not; the only hope is to have contacts with those who *can* be trusted. The payment of protection money to one group gives little protection against another; and both its morality and its wisdom are dubious, to say the least. At government level it can be represented that corruption or infiltration are a greater deterrent to continued development and trade than crime or political terrorism themselves. If none of these approaches is successful, then it is necessary to question whether it is sensible to operate or live in that country at all.

SECURITY AT WORK

By far the most important security measure of all is the security of personnel. If staff are infiltrated or corrupted, all other security precautions—at home and on the road as well as at work—will be compromised.

The background for this must be high staff morale, motivation and training. If staff are proud of their work and of its contribution to the community, are well paid and know that they have as good a job and working conditions as they will get anywhere else, they will resist corruption, and will have an interest in maintaining the operation of their firm. If enough of them feel like that, it will be far more difficult for others to be suborned without being spotted. Much can be achieved by security training. Staff should be alert to suspicious behaviour or undue curiosity by visitors or other staff members in their area of work, and should know what to look for and what to do about it. They should also be trained to observe the security rules themselves.

Vetting of staff is important. Some key personnel will obviously be vetted; but it is easy to overlook others, such as those with access to stores or offices into which weapons or explosives might be smuggled, or in which data about movements or programmes might be acquired.

In any medium- or high-risk situation, staff should be issued with identity cards. In certain circumstances it may be worth using cards with magnetic data, whose details are unknown to the holder, so that security guards who do not know him personally can check that he is who he purports to be.

None of these measures will be effective unless there is a high standard of gate security and a willingness amongst staff to co-operate in being vetted and checked. If there has already been a bombing or a kidnapping, this will be easy; but otherwise it is a matter of briefing and training. The same high standard must be maintained at the entrances to office buildings and over the checking of briefcases, packages and—if necessary—clothing. Acceptance of all these inconveniences depends upon a genuine understanding by the staff of the degree of risk to which they are exposed.

Protection of a high-risk kidnap target should be 'in depth': that is, there should be a series of concentric rings round him wherever he is. These rings may consist of either physical or procedural security, or a combination of the two. None alone is likely to provide a total barrier, but each one can impose delay and give warning. The object is to delay the intruders on the outer rings so that the inner ones can be alerted, and defensive or evasive action taken.

These concentric rings may include: first a general attitude towards security both by those at risk and by other staff; then a perimeter; then a more closely protected area; and a final refuge or 'keep'.

Perimeter security will in any case be needed in large factories or office complexes. Unguarded chain-link fences can be cut within two or three minutes; so other things may be required, such as patrols; dogs; lights; vibratory detectors; acoustic detectors; photoelectric equipment; closed-circuit television (CCTV); radio-link TV; infra-red or microwave beams; or buried-line sensors.

Within the perimeter certain vulnerable areas—including executive offices—may need special protection. Some of the equipment mentioned above may be suitable for this, but there is also shorter-range equipment available, some of which has the advantage of detecting movement in an area rather than in the direct line of a beam. Equipment includes ultrasonic space detectors; thermal scanners; short-range microwave devices; automatic surveillance cameras (these are also valuable for evidence leading to conviction—the best of all deterrents); pressure mats; proximity, impact and anti-tampering devices; metal detectors; and alarm systems.[1]

An executive or official who faces a high risk of kidnapping or assassination should have an office whose windows are not over-

1. For a useful guide to security hardware, see the *Securitech* Catalogue (published by Unisaf, 32–6 Dudley Road, Tunbridge Wells).

looked. He (or his personal staff) should have remote control and identification of entry, secure telephones and alternative communications. He may also need a personal alarm system: a small transmitter with a panic button whose signal can be picked up by sensors in various rooms. These sensors can be the same as those which detect fire, and can, of course, differentiate between an alarm call and a fire signal. The executive's office should be regularly swept for bugging (this can now be done very quickly).[2] He should avoid predictable habits, and keep details of his programme to those who need to know. Above all, his personal staff should not only be carefully vetted, but should be so selected and handled that there is minimum risk of them being bribed or intimidated into co-operation with the terrorists.[3]

SECURITY ON THE ROAD

As was pointed out in Chapter Four, by far the commonest place for a kidnap is on the road between home and work. The most important precautions are to vary the time and route, and to notify the expected time of arrival discreetly to the people at the other end. Wherever possible, wide roads should be chosen, avoiding restrictions such as road works. Cars should be driven as fast as the law permits and in the centre lane, if there is one, to reduce the chances of other vehicles cutting in. The occupants should be alert, and if they see anything suspicious, they should at once turn into a sidestreet; if another car seems to be following, they should drive at best speed to the nearest police station or army post.

It is not easy to vary the route in the immediate vicinity of the home or office, so these are the sites most frequently chosen for kidnapping. If the threat is serious (as it undoubtedly was in the case of Hanns-Martin Schleyer) it may be justifiable to ask the police to move a patrol car to each end of the route at the appro-

2. There are also now various instruments which will detect the arrival of a transmitting device after sweeping.

3. There are technical aids under development which would be able to assist in detecting future deviants as well as past deviants, and these could be used in the same way as a periodic health check.

priate time. Otherwise, a useful tactic is to drive fast past the entrance, looking out for signs of an ambush, and then return.

Drivers should be trained in evasive techniques, such as where to aim at a blocking car so as to push it clear and drive on. Doors should be locked and windows kept shut. Drivers should be suspicious about opening doors or windows if held up (e.g. by a bogus accident, or by people masquerading as policemen). 'Talk windows', like those used at some cash desks, can be installed relatively easily in cars.

Here a dilemma may arise: cars which are best proofed against kidnapping are heavily built and powerful, with drive-on tyres, non-burn and lockable fuel tanks, lockable bonnets and boots, radios, siren alarms and flashing lights. For people facing particularly high risks, they may be armoured. Such cars are both expensive and conspicuous. An alternative, however, is to use inconspicuous cars, which blend into the local traffic. Another useful precaution is for the senior executive to use one of his firm's pool of cars, often changing to a different one. If he uses a chauffeur they should sit together in the front (unless the front passenger seat is already occupied by a bodyguard) and all should be dressed as casually as possible. The choice between a low profile and a heavily guarded and possibly armoured limousine will depend upon the degree of risk—but the least secure combination is a conspicuous vehicle inadequately protected.

If there is an escort car it should travel behind the main car, keeping close on its tail and allowing no other car to cut in. If there are two escort cars, the other one should travel ahead, also close. This, again, has the disadvantage of being conspicuous, but once the low profile alternative has been abandoned, the precautions must balance the threat. Ideally, of course, there should be a third escort car far enough behind not to be caught in the ambush, but able to react quickly. This could have saved Dr Schleyer and Signor Moro, but there is a limit to how many people can be protected to this extent.

Finally, the cars of potential kidnap targets can be fitted with covert cameras, concealed recording devices and electronic tracing devices. The latter can be effective, but they rely on the existence of an adequate tracking organization. This, again, is likely to be available only in the case of major kidnap targets (such as heads of state) or in cities where kidnapping is so prevalent that extreme government countermeasures have to be taken.

If bodyguards are employed, they may provide a false sense of security unless they have been well trained in the skills required to do the job professionally. Inadequately trained bodyguards may even increase the danger, in that they attract attention to the man they are supposed to protect without actually improving his security.

For most ordinary mortals, the best practical approach lies in the low profile, using inconspicuous pool cars (preferably robust), behaving inconspicuously, not publicizing movements, varying the route and timing, selecting routes wisely, keeping all concerned informed, having a good liaison with the police, and learning the techniques of evasion.

HOME AS A FORTRESS

Next to being on the road, the potential victim is most vulnerable at home. As in travel by road, so at home there is a spectrum of security ranging from living in a fortress (or even within a defended compound) to living normally, but taking sensible precautions over avoiding regular movements, admitting visitors, and locking up. Where to pitch home security in this spectrum depends on the appreciation of the threat and the money available. If there is intelligence that a person is a particular target of a determined group, a drastic and expensive change in his lifestyle may be necessary. If, however, he is just one of a number of possible targets, sensible precautions alone may be enough to divert the terrorists to look for a softer target.

In extreme cases, it has sometimes been necessary for senior government officials, diplomats and chief executives to live within a compound with a guarded perimeter, and to move out of it only in convoy. This may, in some cases, be easier and more relaxed for all concerned (including families) than attempting to make an isolated fortress of each individual home. It does, however, depend on a major policy decision by the government, and will therefore be rare.

An individual fortress can be made very strong—though

probably not strong enough to deter a military assault by a large, well armed guerilla unit. But to deter anything short of this, the same defence in depth is necessary as for a factory or office complex: that is, concentric rings to delay and give warning of attack, surrounding a stoutly built house with a 'keep' for protracted defence until help comes.

The outer concentric ring is again a procedural one: the target must avoid predictable routines, and keep knowledge of his movements to those who need to know. The second ring is both procedural and physical: he must not have to expose himself in getting into or out of his car, nor in opening a gate or garage door. As already pointed out, his departure and return are his most vulnerable moments.

The third ring—which becomes the outer ring once he is inside the house—will be an effective perimeter wall, without cover for people to hide close to it, well lit, hard to cross, and with a robust and reliable alarm system built into it.

The fourth ring should be a complete ring of open ground between the perimeter wall and the house. This can be provided by clearing the garden and yard of unnecessary shrubs and hedges. It should be well lit, without shady spots (e.g. behind buildings or trees) in which people can hide. Where special strength is required, the garden can be covered by movement detectors, as described above for 'vulnerable areas' in factories. Buried-line sensors (which can normally cover a perimeter of up to 200 yards) are particularly suitable. There is much to be said for floodlights (or extra floodlights) which are activated by the alarm system either on the perimeter wall or connected to movement detectors covering the garden. A sudden flood of light may catch the intruders by surprise, away from shade, and frighten them into confusion or a withdrawal. The same applies to a loud alarm or siren, with alternative manual and automatic systems of activation.

The doors of the house should, of course, be strong and kept locked, and equipped with means of identifying visitors (CCTV, wide-angled peepholes or mirrors) and remote-controlled opening. (This should also apply to the outer gate of the perimeter which, if it is not manned, should be controlled from the house.)

Entry points should be reduced to a minimum, but alternative exits must be available—e.g. in case of fire, or to enable the family and others to escape while entry is being contested at the main door.

Windows should be shuttered or curtained. If there is a risk of bombing, laminated glass or adhesive polyester film will reduce the risk of flying glass, and wire netting can deflect grenades.

Inside a threatened house there should be an intercom system, alternative telephones (one could be connected directly to the police) and perhaps a radio link. Fire sensors can be adapted also to relay a 'panic button' signal to the police, or to sound a noisy alarm. And—as in a factory or office—the 'keep' should have robust alternative communications, preferably including a battery radio transmitter which can be netted to the police frequency.

Once again, a corrupt or treacherous member of the household can nullify all other defensive measures. A terrorist group after a particular victim will without doubt try to infiltrate his household or personal staff, or to bribe or coerce them. Particular care should be taken in vetting servants to ensure that they are not vulnerable to blackmail or intimidation—possibly through threats to their families. The history of kidnapping and assassination is full of examples of staff who wished to be loyal but succumbed to threats against their families.

SECURITY IN AN ORDINARY HOME

But not everyone can afford to live in a fortress. The above system, in full, requires the resources of a millionaire or a large corporation, and even a large corporation could provide it only for a few.

For the rest, the aim must be to avoid being chosen as an easy target. The demands need not be impossible. Predictable habits and an ostentatious profile must be avoided. A house should be chosen in a suitable area, without concealed access for intruders, and with neighbours who can be relied upon to help. Access to the garage from within the house and a remote-controlled garage door will do much to reduce the danger at the two worst moments. There must be strict attention to locking up and drawing cur-

D

tains. There should be a chain on the door; and there should preferably be some means of recognizing the visitors before even unlocking the door, and certainly before releasing the chain. The opening of the door is a very vulnerable moment, and the person opening it should not allow himself to be a visible target until he has positively identified the visitors. If they claim to be friends of a member of the family, they should not be admitted without identification by that member of the family, unless they are precisely as expected. If they claim to be, say, policemen or electricians, a telephone call should be made to their headquarters before the door is released. If there are children or servants, they too must be briefed to be strict about this. The vetting of servants has already been mentioned. And a really faithful dog—of a suitably frightening breed—can be the best guardian and the best deterrent of all, because an intruder knows that he can argue with a man but not with a dog.

THE FAMILY

Difficult problems arise over families, because the kidnapping of a beloved wife or child may well lead a man who would readily hazard his own life to give way to a threat to theirs.

Wives may have jobs in which they cannot hope for 'concentric rings' of protection; or they may want to lead an active social life which they feel contributes to their husband's success. Some may like to drive around in conspicuous sports cars. They may not appreciate the hazard either to themselves or to their husbands, who will have to handle the crisis if they are kidnapped. Hard decisions may be necessary. If their life becomes too restricted in a high-risk area, it may be better for everyone's peace of mind for them to move away (as soldiers' wives have to leave an operational area)—but a top executive may himself refuse to work in the country if it means the splitting of his family.

Children of school age should never be needlessly exposed. They should be escorted to and from school, and the school should have strict instructions never to hand them over to any unauthorized person who claims to have come to collect them.

As with their parents, their most dangerous moments are on the road or at the gates of their school or their home.

Older teenagers and children at university may present a particular problem. They may themselves be politically subverted without realizing that the real purpose is the kidnapping or assassination of their parents. Or they may unwittingly make friends with fellow students who intend to use their friendship for that purpose. Such a 'friend', once admitted, can breach defences more effectively than the most heavily armed intruder (see page 38).

INSURANCE

The wisdom and ethics of kidnap insurance are frequently questioned on the grounds that the existence of such insurance will make the insured person a more likely target, and remove his incentive to recover the money; that it will make the payment of a ransom more likely; and that ransoms will be paid more quickly, and will be larger. In fact, the reverse is true. All available evidence suggests that insurance, by introducing a professional element into both security precautions and negotiations, reduces the chance of being kidnapped, reduces the size of the ransom (if paid at all) ensures co-operation with the police, and increases their chance of arresting the kidnappers by extending the period of negotiation—just as fire insurance reduces the risk of fire.

Lloyd's, who have for many years covered the bulk of kidnap insurance worldwide, insist on certain conditions. First, the existence of the policy must be kept secret. Second, the police must be informed. If either of these conditions is broken, the policy becomes invalid—just as insurance against theft is invalidated if the police are not notified immediately. Thus the risk that negotiators will keep the police in the dark and settle immediately for the full ransom demanded by the kidnapper— as has happened in so many kidnappings—is almost wholly removed.

Lloyd's issue only policies of indemnity, and those are limited to the sum which the firm or individual can pay from their own resources, and which they can then reclaim from the under-

writers (less an agreed excess) provided that the conditions have
been fulfilled. They cannot borrow against the security of the
policy, since this would infringe the secrecy clause and thereby
invalidate it. By insisting (like other kinds of insurer) on proper
security measures, averting panic settlements by increasing the
information and time available to the police, the underwriters
reduce ransoms and assist arrests and convictions—as well as
saving the victim and his family or firm from catastrophic losses
and debts.

SECURITY FIRMS AND ADVISERS

Lloyd's employ experienced professional advisers—at the expense of the underwriters—to assess and reduce the risk. As with
fire and theft insurance, if the client acts upon their advice, his
premiums may be reduced. These advisers can, if preferred, be
engaged directly by a client whether he wishes to insure or not.

In either case, the adviser carries out a detailed survey of the
risk and submits specific recommendations for reducing it. In
the event of an actual kidnap, he can be called upon to advise on
crisis management and negotiating—again paid either by the
underwriters or by an uninsured client. Since underwriters have
at least as great an incentive as the victim or his associates to
avoid or minimize the ransom, and to see kidnappers appre-
hended to deter others, their advisers have unique experience
in both security precautions and crisis management. At the time
of writing they are believed to have advised in the post-kidnap
negotiations in over fifty cases in Latin America and Europe, in
addition to their main task of carrying out security surveys.
Families and firms, distraught and bewildered by the suddenness
of the blow, faced with a situation of which they have no previous
experience, have benefited both financially and psychologically
from their help—as have police forces in bringing about arrests
and convictions. The subject of crisis management and negotiation will be examined in more detail in Chapter Nine.

There are many security firms, all over the world, who can
provide guards, and advise upon and install security hardware.
Firms may be chosen by reference to the British Security

Industry Association, or employed as a result of a survey by an independent adviser, with whom there is then a three-cornered relationship—as there is between a client, architect and builder, or between a public authority, consulting engineer and contractor. No security firm or adviser, unless they have a proven public reputation, should be engaged without checking with the police, not only to ensure against infiltration, treachery or corruption, but also because security in the event of attack depends upon the closest co-operation and confidence between the security firms and the police. In Britain, the police crime prevention officer will carry out a survey free of charge if requested, and he can be asked for his opinion on the various security firms and security advisers available.

Chapter Eight

Survival as a Hostage

BEING MENTALLY PREPARED

BEFORE considering contingency planning and crisis management, it is important to understand the ordeal of the hostage, because the negotiator must all the time try to visualize what is happening to him, and how he may be reacting.

The hostage will have more chance of survival if he is mentally prepared. The shock of being kidnapped will probably be the worst he ever has to endure. A busy, comfortable, gregarious and secure existence, in which he is always exercising options and getting a response, will suddenly be transformed into a forced inactivity and isolation, with no options at all, and great discomfort and degradation. The transformation will have been violent, and he will have been pushed around and possibly injured. He may have seen his driver or bodyguards killed trying to defend him. He will find himself stripped to his underwear, forced to ask for a bucket in which to perform his bodily functions in full view of people who seem to take a conscious delight in humiliating him. Worst of all will be fear, and particularly fear of the unknown. He does not know whether he will be tortured or killed, or if so, when. The ordeal is open-ended. And it will be made worse by self-pity or reproach: 'why me?', 'if only ...' The first few hours will perhaps be the most horrible hours in his life.

He will endure the ordeal better if he has thought about it rationally, but not morbidly. Depending upon how seriously he regards the threat and the character of those involved, he will gain from having discussed the possibility of kidnap with his wife or his colleagues. Geoffrey Jackson did so with both, and with the Foreign Office in London. His book is truly valuable reading for anyone facing a high risk.

The more the victim knows about kidnapping, the less will be the fear of the unknown. He will be able to remind himself that only about 3 per cent of kidnap victims have been killed in cold blood (though more have been killed during the snatch or in rescue attempts); and that, though some hostages are held for a long time (one was held for twenty-two months before being released on payment of a ransom), the majority of kidnaps have ended in under five days.[1] And—albeit cold comfort—he can recall that, if it does last longer, the human body and spirit have remarkable powers of adaptation, and that the great majority of hostages have survived without permanent damage.

Soldiers with duties classed as 'prone to capture' (e.g. in stay-behind parties, parachute units or deep penetration patrols) go through a basic programme of training to prepare them for the ordeal. This includes simulation of treatment at capture (often painfully realistic), isolation, acute discomfort, degradation, and mental disorientation. All who have done this testify to its value. Even if the ordeal has only been faced mentally, the victim at least knows what to expect, and it will be easier to bear.

THE SNATCH

The moment of kidnap offers the best—and perhaps the only— chance of escape. Evasive driving has already been mentioned. A high-risk potential victim (or his driver) is more likely to grasp this fleeting opportunity if he has run through some scenarios in his mind, perhaps as he drives to and from work. The basis of these scenarios should be to do what the kidnappers least expect, as the best way of throwing them off their stride.

Curtis Cutter, US consul general in Porto Allegre, Brazil, thwarted a late-night kidnapping attempt outside his home in April 1970, when a car blocked his path and four armed men jumped out. He drove straight at the men, carrying one of them along on his bumper for several yards. The others fired and Cutter was wounded, but he escaped.

It was perhaps with this in mind that, when Hanns-Martin

1. Brian Jenkins, *Hostage Survival: Some Preliminary Observations* and Corporation, Santa Monica, 1976).

Schleyer's car was blocked by the terrorists' minibus in September 1977, the 'gap' was filled by a girl terrorist pushing a pram off the pavement. She knew that few drivers would run down a baby, and the hesitation proved fatal to the driver, the body guards and, in the end, to Schleyer himself.

Sometimes, particularly in a more lawless society, in which they know that witnesses will not dare to come forward, the kidnappers may deliberately pick a crowded street for the holdup, to give themselves more time and cover. Few policemen or body-guards would fire unhesitatingly at a man amongst a crowd of innocent bystanders. In one Latin-American capital the victim's car was rammed by another in a long, narrow, crowded shopping street. The two drivers both got out and a long altercation ensued. The victim got out and joined in. By this time a large crowd had gathered round, amongst which were the other kidnappers (who had meanwhile signalled their other cars to block both ends of the street). Only when they were quite sure that all was set up and that they had got the right man did they produce their guns and bundle him into a car.

Once his car has been stopped and the victim finds himself facing armed men, there is little he can do. Unless police or bodyguards are still fighting to open an escape route, the only sensible course is usually to surrender and do what the terrorists say. Heroics achieve nothing unless there is a real chance of success.

THE FIRST FEW DAYS

The victim should, from the moment of his capture, make a determined effort to recover his calm and alertness so that he can start making mental notes of any details likely to help the police. He will be able to compose himself more quickly if he avoids provoking his kidnappers. He should do his utmost to fix in his mind their faces, voices, dress and characteristics; how many they were; and the particulars of any vehicles that were involved. If psychologically prepared, he will be better able to discipline himself, to concentrate on these things rather than on agonizing over why it happened.

He will probably be forced face down on to the floor of the car so that he cannot see, and he may later be transferred into a closed van, or have his eyes covered and his ears plugged. Nevertheless, he should fix in his mind any clues he can get about his route: time, speed, distance, sharp turns, gradients, traffic lights etc.; and any sights or sound he is able to detect, such as crossing a railway or passing close to the airport; also the direction of the sun. If he has an idea whether he went north or south, he may possibly find a way of communicating this during negotiations, or in written or taped messages he is ordered to send out; even if he cannot do that, the information may help in arresting the gang later.

He should also try to detect the kind of place into which he is taken: e.g. into a garage with inside access to a suburban house, the car park under a block of flats, the back entrance of a shop, or a workshop or a warehouse. If the gang is a professional one, the likeliest eventual hideout (probably after at least one transfer between vehicles, and perhaps also after a brief spell in a transit lockup) will be a house, flat or garage in a quiet, prosperous suburb, which may offer more choices of getaway route than an isolated farmhouse. Again, the victim should consciously store sights, sounds and smells in his memory. At least one hostage contributed to the eventual capture of his kidnappers because he could hear aircraft taking off from a small and recognizable airfield; and another by remembering details of the wallpaper.

The treatment of the victim in the first few days after capture is likely to be at its most brutal, calculated to humiliate and demoralize. He may be injected with some drug such as scopolamine, designed to relax resistance and loosen the tongue. Geoffrey Jackson countered this drug by disciplining himself to talk fluently to the point of verbosity on unimportant issues and, if cornered on important ones, to attempt to blur his answers with more verbosity, in such a way as to make the two indistinguishable.

Interrogators are likely (as described in Chapter Four) to use Pavlovian techniques of contrasting brutality and kindness, light and dark, noise and silence; and to attempt mental disorientation by sensory deprivation, probably keeping the victim permanently blindfolded, with ears plugged, without any means

of telling the time of day, with deliberately irregular and unpleasant food (perhaps none at all for a time) and repeated
interruption of sleep (if any). He can only steel himself to endure
it, knowing that this is probably going to be the worst time of all,
reminding himself again and again that the great majority of
hostages survive.

He must be particularly careful not to reveal, unwittingly,
anything about the likely reactions to his capture. He will probably be asked for a telephone number to ring; and he should
think about who is likely to react best to the first message—
because this first reaction can influence all subsequent negotiations. He should also avoid discussion about how ransom money
might be raised, or to give any clue which will help the kidnappers to gauge the level at which to pitch their first demand.
The only exception to this is that he could consider feeding in
any genuine reasons why the sum the kidnappers are demanding
could not conceivably be found—but this is a dangerous subject,
and he may do better to avoid it if he can.

He must do his utmost to restore his own morale. Post-kidnap
shock is a major physiological and psychological problem; and
the fact that (unlike a soldier or a pilot in war) he may be wholly
unprepared for it makes it worse. The kidnappers will do their
utmost to exploit this in order to establish total dominance over
him; and he must consciously resist that, not by heroics and
provocation, but by battling to retain his self-respect and sense
of humour. Geoffrey Jackson had his kidnappers laughing within
minutes of his kidnapping by accusing them of trying to tattoo
the Tupamaro emblem on his hand as they tried to inject him
with a drug during the first bumpy car ride. He also took the
offensive, though not provocatively, by telling them that he had
already agreed with the British and Uruguayan governments that
they would make no concessions of any kind to secure his release.

SURVIVING THE LONG NIGHT

Surviving the Long Night is the apt title of the US edition of
Jackson's book. Though most kidnaps end within a few days, the
victim will do well to face the possibility of a longer ordeal. Again,

his most vital task is to maintain his self-respect—and his physical and mental health. The kidnappers will still try to prevent this, but they may gradually relax. Most criminals retain a vestige of humanity which they cannot wholly stifle, though some fanatical political terrorists have none. (A chilling example of this is given in Chapter Twelve.) The Japanese Red Army terrorists are specifically trained to stifle their human reactions and not to allow any softening of their attitude, either to victims or, if they are besieged, to negotiators.

The rapport which often develops between kidnappers and their victims is now well known, and its psychological roots are fully established. Provided that it does not lead him to give away vital information or encourage his kidnappers to hold out for a higher ransom, the victim should not resist the development of this rapport, but foster it. The more it develops, the less likely they are to kill him. (See Chapter Sixteen for the rather touching farewell to a victim being dumped on the roadside by one of his guards who, as a rank-and-file criminal, had retained more than a vestige of humanity.)

The hostage's greatest enemy is demoralization by inactivity and morbid contemplation. He should do his utmost to find positive things to do, within the limitations available to him. Exercise programmes (like the Canadian Air Force 5BX system) can be done in any space in which a man can stand up and lie down. Mental exercises, such as memorizing details of his cell; or composing a diary or letter to be written later or (Jackson again) short stories, or verses; or designing the ideal home; or trying to memorize plays, poetry or music, can keep the mind from unhealthier thoughts. Planning escapes, however unlikely, may help, and soldiers are trained to start doing this—for psychological reasons—from the moment they are captured.

Provocative non-co-operation is likely to be counterproductive, but the victim may be able to restore his own morale by little victories such as persuading his captors to allow him a pencil and paper, or to alter a phrase in a letter or taped statement which they are compelling him to send out.

The problem of providing written or taped communications is a difficult one. On the whole, it is best to give them fairly freely. Some men will prefer to resist making statements which could be of propaganda value to their enemies; and all should certainly avoid saying anything which will give away important secrets, or put someone else's life at risk. Apart from this, however, resistance may not be worth the price in exacerbation of the captor-hostage relationship. Statements will be recognized by everyone as being made under duress, and will carry no weight. On the positive side, they will help the police and the negotiators to judge the hostage's state of mind, either from his recorded tone of voice, or from analysis of his handwriting by graphologists.

It is possible to agree in advance upon some system of code-words whose use can transmit a particular meaning; but they are probably of limited value. The victim may not know much worth communicating; he may find it difficult to arrange their inclusion without exciting suspicion; and the kidnappers may, deliberately or accidentally, dictate the inclusion of a word which sends a dangerously misleading message.

The conditions of a hostage are calculated to develop total dependence upon his captors. According to their whim, he eats or starves, sleeps or wakes, washes or urinates. He reverts to the relationship of a baby to its mother. His captors can assume the mantle of gods, with (literally) the power of life or death over him. This can be totally demoralizing, especially if the 'gods' are young enough to be his children and their doctrinaire opinions or lifestyle represent all that he despises. Nevertheless, provided that it is recognized, this relationship can be handled in such a way as to develop a constructive rapport, and to weaken the fanaticism and inhumanity of the kidnappers—because the effect works both ways.

SIEGE AND RESCUE

If the police discover where the hostage is being held, and can surround it or raid it before he is moved away, a totally new situation arises, psychologically and physically.

The handling of such a situation by police and negotiators is examined in Chapter Ten. The victim can play an important part, both in getting information out to the police, and in influencing the actions of his guards.

The police will be playing for time. One of the effects of this may be the intensification of the rapport between kidnappers and hostages, because they now share the same ordeal. Since the greatest threat to all their lives has become the guns of the police, the hostage may find himself identifying with his captors. He must not allow this feeling to go too far, but it can be helpful to the extent that it further reduces the likelihood of their killing him. He can subtly remind them that, once he is dead, they have not only played their last card, but they have also removed the only insurance they have against the police wading in with guns, grenades or incendiary devices to kill every one of them.

The victim's best course is to do his utmost to calm them, lest they go berserk and kill both him and themselves, and to help spin out the negotiations. He should try both to weaken their resistance and to help to wear them out, physically and mentally. Their position of dominance has been destroyed. He can remind them, kindly if possible, that they can achieve nothing if they are dead, politically or otherwise; and that as kidnappers they have already forfeited all hope of being regarded by the public as martyrs. He may even feel a genuine desire to promise to do his best to reduce their sentences.

He should not agree to negotiate with the police in place of the kidnappers, since the process of negotiation with them gives the police and their psychiatric advisers the best hope of judging their state of mind. He should remember that, if the police know their job, they will have established surveillance microphones very soon after the siege is mounted. He should avoid reminding his captors of this, but should take whatever chances he can to direct the conversation in ways likely to help those who are trying to rescue him.

If the kidnap ends with an armed rescue—whether after a siege or by a surprise raid—the hostage must help the police both to save his life and to capture the kidnappers. The police share these aims, so they will almost certainly shout instructions to him. These will probably be to lie down, keep still, and identify himself (if he is wise he will already have tried to communicate, through the bug or otherwise, how he is dressed). And, of course, it will be in everyone's interest if he can persuade the kidnappers to yield quietly.

Chapter Nine

Contingency Planning and Crisis Management

CONTINGENCY PLANNING AT VARIOUS LEVELS

SECURITY precautions (see Chapter Seven) are aimed to deter a kidnap attempt, or to prevent it from succeeding. Contingency planning covers the action to be taken if a kidnapping does occur: crisis management; negotiation; release of the victim; and detection and arrest of the kidnappers.

For a firm or family threatened by kidnapping the priorities in contingency planning are: first, the release of the victim at the lowest possible cost—if possible at no cost at all; second, the prevention of supplementary kidnapping of his colleagues or members of his family; and third, the arrest of the kidnappers, either before or after the victim is released. The police will, of course, normally put the last of these priorities first, though they will still share all three aims.

Contingency planning should be done simultaneously with security planning, as the two plans must be linked. The security adviser engaged for a survey should, wherever possible, be one who can at the same time help to make a contingency plan; and, in the event of a kidnap, can be called in to advise during crisis management and negotiation.

There may be up to five different levels of contingency planning, ranging from international down to individual.

At the international level, there should be plans for bilateral exchange of intelligence (both as a matter of routine and during an incident) and for extradition of terrorists (see pages 78–9). Expatriate firms may be able to further these through their own embassies.

At the national level, the government must co-ordinate security planning between its own departments, the police and other security forces, the legislature, the judiciary, industry and vulnerable individuals (see pages 79–80).

There may be a multinational corporate headquarters level, at which policies for security (including financial allocation for it) and for crisis management are necessary, with particular attention to delegation of powers to subsidiaries and communication with them.

The level of the firm on the ground, whether independent or subsidiary, expatriate or locally based, is where the bulk of the detailed planning must be done. That is the main content of this chapter.

The individual may be involved as a member of a firm, or as an official (in government or in an embassy); or, if he is a target by reason of his personal wealth, he may have to deal directly with the police and others in his planning. In that case, the principles are generally the same as for the firm, though with a greater emphasis on his home and his family.

As was pointed out in Chapter Five, the interests of those involved may conflict. To recapitulate briefly: the potential victim has to balance the risk against the cost and inconvenience of reducing it, and he has to decide how to apply this to his family; lawyers, advisers and security firms will owe their first loyalty to their clients, so far as is consistent with their responsibility as citizens; a corporate headquarters will be concerned with the effect of the handling of a crisis on its subsidiaries, on its image, on its legal obligations, on its staff morale and on its finances; the firm on the ground has similar cares, but may live under different laws from its head office and have different priorities, with staff morale predominant; the police and the army may be concerned more with making arrests than with saving lives, though they know that they will defeat their own ends if they thereby lose the co-operation of the victim's family or firm; the government, the legislature and the judiciary are concerned with upholding the law and their own credibility, and with the effect of a particular crisis on their future; overseas governments are concerned about their nationals and about future relations with the host government; and the media are concerned with news, with not being scooped, and with their public image.

Joint Planning with the Police

The police must be brought into contingency plans. Even where it is known that some policemen are corrupt, the great majority will not be. Every effort must be made to identify these, through government, diplomatic or other sources, and to confine contact to those who can be trusted. It may be wise to keep certain information strictly on a 'need to know' basis, as the police undoubtedly will themselves. But if the entire police force were corrupt, there would be no point in contingency planning anyway. The only recipe for survival would be to pay protection money to the organizations posing the threat, and this would not be a viable policy for very long.

The first field of co-operation is over intelligence. If the police are to share any of their information, they will not only need to be sure about discretion and security, but also to have the prospect of a worthwhile return of information in exchange. If such information comes from independent sources, it should not be shared without their knowledge and approval. Nothing dries up intelligence more quickly than the suspicion that it will be indiscreetly passed on.

The most delicate information is about the *sources* of intelligence, and that should be neither asked nor shared. Much of the intelligence itself, however, may not be too sensitive, provided that its knowledge does not in itself give a clue to its source. Information about criminal and terrorist movements, their strength and organization, their finances, their armament, their methods and their degree of public support (or acceptance) in various areas can be shared with reasonable discretion; this may include the pattern of previous incidents, of how many victims have been killed (and why), and of the average levels of ransom demands and settlements. Patterns may vary greatly between cities and between countries. The pattern in Northern Ireland is clearly very different from that in England. In Italy, most kidnap victims are Italians, whereas in Argentina many are expatriates. In Guatemala, in addition to kidnapping itself, there is a prevalence of extortion of protection money under the threat of kidnapping. In Germany, the victims of political kidnapping and assassination have been carefully selected for their impact on the national and world media, and for the anticipated degree of provocation to the government to overreact. One could quote similar contrasts for other countries; and it is obvious folly to make contingency plans in one country based upon a too generalized conception of the threat, or upon a threat which is relevant only to another country.

A firm will also be wise to take a dispassionate look at itself through terrorist eyes. Have there been threats or incidents in the past? What is its public image? Is it generally recognized—or disliked—as a foreign-based concern? Will the kidnapping of one of its members have a publicity impact locally and in the world? What is likely to be the local public reaction: 'serve them right', or 'this could threaten our jobs', or what? What is public knowledge—or belief—about its finances, or those of its parent corporation? Are its labour relations, past or present, a factor? A close and frank relationship with the police can contribute a great deal to a realistic self-assessment.

The second main area of co-operation with the police is in agreement on procedures in the event of an attack or of a kidnap message being received. Whom should the company (or family) inform? Would the police provide a checklist of the kind of information they require? How can the police best be called without the kidnappers knowing? Should any direct or secure communications—e.g. a direct telephone link or alarm link to the police—be set up in advance? Should there be a contingency plan for setting up additional communications in the event of an incident? Tape recorders? Telephone tapping? How do the police suggest that the media should be handled? What are the prospects of a fraudulent kidnapping; and how can it best be detected? Are there any particular aspects of the law which the company should watch?

DETAILED PLANS FOR CRISIS MANAGEMENT

A firm which makes a contingency plan against kidnapping should maintain a confidential personal file for any of its executives who is a possible target. This should include his address and telephone number; particulars of his wife and children and of their schools and regular activities (e.g. dancing class on Tuesdays); numbers of their passports, credit cards, identity cards, etc.; details of their car or cars; the names, addresses and telephone numbers of their doctor and lawyer, and of close neighbours or trusted friends; full medical data for an emergency, including blood groups of all the family, any special problems (weak heart, slipped disc, diabetes) and any drugs which may be needed; also an up-to-date photograph, samples of handwriting and voice recordings, which after a kidnapping may assist in assessing the victim's health and state of mind.

The firm should establish a shadow crisis management team, which should prepare the contingency plans and meet regularly to review them. The chief executive should not be chairman of the team, first because he should be detached, and second because he is the likeliest victim himself; but he should be free to attend meetings when he chooses. There should be an alternative chairman of the team, which should normally include the chief security officer, the insurance or risk manager, the financial director, a legal adviser, an executive concerned with public relations, and the man most likely to be charged with negotiation in the event of a kidnap. The selection of the negotiator is discussed later in this chapter.

An important part of the task of this team is to be ready to receive and react to a threat or to a kidnap message, and to ensure that all members of staff who might receive such a message are briefed as to how to react to it. A suitable pro forma for this may be combined with one for receipt of a bomb threat. Staff receiving a kidnap message should be instructed *not* to inform the police immediately, because the kidnappers will undoubtedly warn them not to, and an indiscreet call could hazard the victim's life. The person receiving the message should, however, notify one of a number of named executives; and that executive should inform the particular officer or office in accordance with procedure agreed with the police in advance.

NEGOTIATION

The choice of the principal negotiator is probably the most important single decision of the crisis management team. He should have practical experience of negotiation and bargaining; so a lawyer, or someone concerned with labour relations, may be most suitable. He should not normally be an expatriate, though he can be if he speaks the language fluently, and is sufficiently familiar with local customs and geography. He must be determined, persuasive, intelligent, calm, discreet, patient and detached; and must be able to use his initiative without departing from his instructions.

He must act under instructions (preferably always given by the same person) because he must *not* be made personally responsible for taking the most important decisions; and he should not be emotionally involved (i.e. he should not be a close friend or relation of the victim). He must be able to play for time by saying that he has to refer to the family or firm. He should be fully briefed, and if necessary rehearsed (preferably by an adviser experienced in kidnap negotiations) before each telephone call expected from the kidnappers. He should *not* have to worry about how far he can go; he should know how far (e.g. not to agree to pay more than a stated maximum, or to insist on payment in local currency) before he starts, so that he can concentrate his whole mind on negotiating the best deal he can within those limits.

One or more reserve negotiators should be earmarked and kept in the picture, in case the principal negotiator is not available, or in case it becomes tactically desirable to change the voice.

Negotiation is most commonly conducted by a kidnapper telephoning an agreed number from a callbox (because this is the most difficult to trace). It may, however, be done by letter from the kidnappers, who require the negotiator to reply, say, by an advertisement in a local newspaper, using a code (e.g. he may be told to offer a car for sale, giving a price in lire which will be interpreted as his offer in US dollars).

The establishment of a reliable channel of communication, in which the kidnappers themselves gain confidence, is an early requirement. The police must be kept informed. All telephone calls must be taped and logged. The kidnappers will assume that this is so and will probably also assume that the line is being tapped by the police, though they may use or require certain stratagems to make this difficult. Because of the risk of the call being traced, the caller may insist on ringing off after about two minutes. It is therefore essential that the negotiator is fully ready for the call, with notes of what he means to say.

Two fundamentals in negotiation are to ensure that those on the other end really are the kidnappers, and not another gang trying to get their hands on the ransom; and that the victim is still alive. For this purpose, frequent proof questions are needed. This will normally comprise questions to which only the victim can know the answer; or they may require a tape of his voice reading an extract from the current issue of a morning paper; or a photograph of him (sent through the post) holding a copy of that paper; or a letter in his handwriting which, from its content (e.g. mention of a current news item) could only have been written on that day. An experienced kidnapper will appreciate that such a proof call will be required immediately negotiation begins, and at periodic intervals, and certainly at the very end, a few hours before any ransom is paid.

Particular care must be taken not to give information which could put some other member of the family or firm at risk. Supplementary kidnappings are not uncommon where negotiations are protracted. These not only compound the problem, but also greatly increase the danger of one of the two victims being killed, as the kidnappers will still have the other one left as a card in their hand. As regards the family, the best course is for them to leave the area as soon as possible after the kidnap, though the wife, in particular, may be reluctant to do so. It should, however, be a reassurance to the victim to know that she is somewhere safe; and there should be no insurmountable problems about getting questions and answers for proof calls, even if she is far away.

It would be inappropriate to say too much about the techniques of coercive bargaining. Much has been learned from kidnaps in recent years. Suffice it to say that the kidnappers will do their utmost to precipitate a panic settlement by threats to the victim's life, which they are most unlikely to carry out unless their aim is to kill him as a warning to others; if they become frightened or lose hope of getting anything at all, they might, however, cut their losses and do it. The second major point is that, though they are all-powerful in relation to their victim, they are essentially weak; they are in the position of hunted animals, for whom death or captivity is virtually certain if they are spotted; as each day goes by the threat of discovery and failure increases, yet they are reluctant to throw away their last card; their nervousness and exhaustion will therefore increase; this will become intense when they think that a ransom is almost within their grasp, and they will become more and more anxious to settle. At that stage, a good negotiator will have turned the tables, and will be in the psychologically dominant position.

Chapter Ten

Release by Ransom, Siege or Raid

PAYING A RANSOM

IDEALLY, negotiations should give the police sufficient time to locate the hideout, and the victim's release can then be secured by a siege or a raid. These will be examined later in the chapter; but there are occasions when it must be decided to pay a ransom, without losing sight of the opportunity this offers for the detection and arrest of the kidnappers, either during or after their collection of the money.

It is possible that the kidnappers may try to have the money paid in hard currency in a foreign country, either into a number of different bank accounts (e.g. in Switzerland or the USA, or in a country where currency regulations are lax), or possibly dumped in cash for collection by accomplices there (in which case the methods may be similar to those for local currency—see below). Though theoretically attractive for the kidnapper, these measures are complicated and run a higher risk of detection in the end—assuming reasonable international co-operation.

Where the payment is to be within the country of the kidnap, the kidnappers may still demand it in hard currency—most commonly in US dollars. This will again complicate their problems; but if they can once get it out of the country, it will be harder to trace, even assuming that the numbers of some or all of the notes have been recorded, because there will be a wider choice of countries in which such currencies will be accepted without demur than for local currency (such as lire or pesos). Much will depend on the strictness of baggage checks out of the kidnap country and into the ones selected for disposal of the money.

Most kidnappers in fact settle for payment in local currency, but specify that it must be in well worn notes of low denomination, not with consecutive numbers. This is because blocks of numbers are easily noted, whereas the recording of the numbers of all the notes in two suitcases full of bundles of used notes would be a prodigious task. Photographing them may be the quickest answer. Even then, however, it will be hard to keep track of low denomination notes unless the kidnappers try to change them in too much of a hurry.

To gather together large numbers of such notes takes quite a long time; and the negotiator may have to persuade the kidnappers to allow for this, and to warn them that undue haste in assembling suspiciously large sums is likely to increase the chances of detection. At this stage the kidnappers will be especially sensitive about police surveillance, and will repeatedly demand guarantees that the whole process is being kept secret. They will use every kind of threat and stratagem to ensure this (for example, by demanding a change of the negotiator's telephone at short notice). There is a particular risk of a supplementary kidnap in this period— though, if the negotiators and police are alert, this presents greater hazards to the kidnappers.

Meanwhile, volunteers will have to be found to drop the money (these will hereafter be referred to as the 'droppers'). There is likely to be no great rush of volunteers for this task; and this must be explained firmly to the kidnappers if they try to specify who the droppers should be.

The negotiator, however, is now in a stronger position than before, because the kidnappers will be in a state of high tension, and probably anxious to end the business quickly. The negotiator can therefore become very firm over *his* conditions. These must include the requirement that proof of identification is presented at the handover to ensure that those collecting the money really are those who are holding the victim (e.g. by producing the victim's passport or credit card) and that there is incontrovertible proof that the victim is alive immediately before the droppers draw out the money and set out for the rendezvous (RV).

Having agreed upon a sum, upon the currency and denominations, and upon the first stage of the drop (e.g. by two people in a car whose particulars are stated) and upon the earliest time by which they will be ready, the negotiator will receive a message giving the first RV. This may be sent in a note (e.g. with a bunch of flowers); or by telephone, with every possible device to guard against police tapping. The RV will probably be some semi-public place in which police surveillance will be particularly difficult and surveillance by the kidnappers relatively easy—for example in a bar in a poor quarter of town, at a quiet period when strangers would easily be spotted. Only when they are sure that there is no police surveillance will they send the next message—perhaps by calling one of the droppers to the telephone under a previously agreed name. This will say where the next clue in the treasure hunt is to be found (e.g. behind a lavatory cistern in the toilet at the back of the bar). There will probably be a series of such RVs and clues, in bars, kiosks, car parks etc., each similarly designed to guard against police surveillance. The route between them may include irregular turnings at which they hope to spot if a police car is following, and also sometimes a switch of cars. Examples are given in Chapters Eleven, Fourteen and Sixteen. The eventual handover may be by the droppers' car being waylaid at a point with secure getaways; or by an instruction that they are to park the car at a stated spot with the key in place and the money in the boot, and to walk back into town, presumably covered by guns, without turning their heads. The negotiator, however, should have insisted that the money will in no circumstances be delivered unless the identification (victim's passport etc.) is received, either at the handover itself or with one of the clues.

The drop is an intensely sensitive process, so there is a serious risk that, if the kidnappers sense police surveillance, they may abandon it and demand more severe terms, and the negotiations will almost certainly be extended. They may even kill the victim *pour encourager les autres*, and start again with another victim. For this reason the police must themselves be forebearing. It may well pay them in the end to promise the negotiator not to interfere, and rely on him to give them all possible help afterwards in detection. Otherwise, the victim's family (whether his ransom is being paid by them or by his firm) may insist on the final negotiation of the drop being done behind the backs of the police. The likely police response to this may be to try to ambush the droppers or to arrest the negotiator—and in that case the kidnappers will have enormously increased their chances by turning their opponents at each other's throats at the critical moment. A desperate family may then settle quickly and secretly.

If the police do attempt surveillance of the drop—with or without the negotiator's co-operation—they must use the utmost discretion. A car with a recognizable police profile (e.g. with radio aerials, or obvious police officers in it) could be fatal not only to the victim but also to the droppers. Despite the obvious anxiety of the victim's family at this point, they must appreciate that the drop offers the police their best opportunity to identify the kidnappers.

The best way for this problem to be handled is—as in every other aspect of contingency planning and crisis management—with the frankest possible relationship between the negotiator and the police, and with the police accepting that surveillance of the type they would like, or even for surveillance at all, may be counterproductive to their own as well as to the victim's interests. Certainly, the public will be quick to blame them if a stereotyped 'big-booted policeman blunders in', and gets the victim killed. Patience, discretion and forebearance, even at the expense of short-term hopes of arrest, are likely to be the most productive in the end. Chapters Fourteen and Sixteen give good examples of this.

SIEGES

If the location of the hideout is detected, either during the negotiations or between the payment of a ransom and the release of the victim, the nature of the situation is radically changed. First, the matter will thereafter be handled by the police or the army; and second, the negotiator, presumably now a police officer with psychiatric advice available to him, should quickly be able to establish psychological dominance over the kidnappers. Their roles, in fact, are reversed. The kidnappers become the prisoners—even though they hold a hostage within the prison.

Most siege situations have ended successfully, with the release of the great majority of the hostages alive, and with the arrest of the kidnappers: e.g. by the Dutch at Scheveningen and Assen and in the South Moluccan train hijackings; by the British at

Spaghetti House and Balcome Street; by the Irish in the case of
Dr Herrema; by the Swedes in the Stockholm bank siege; and
by the New York police in the siege of Black Muslims in Brook-
lyn in 1973. So have raids, such as at Entebbe and Mogadishu.

A number of these incidents are examined in the case studies
in Part IV.

Unless the kidnappers can be surprised and overwhelmed in
the first few minutes (in which case it is a raid rather than a siege),
the essence of the successful siege is patience. It is in three stages:
containment, negotiation and release. The containment is the
most dangerous moment. Kidnappers are not, by nature, particularly stable or rational people. If they are rushed, they may go
berserk, turning upon their victim and probably then upon
themselves.

For the same reason, care should be taken not to use force too
soon, or to escalate it too quickly. Once any particular level of
force has been reached, it is hard to reduce it. The most dangerous
period will have passed when the kidnappers decide that the
thing they want most is to get out alive. A psychiatrist may be
able to identify this moment. Thereafter the aim should be to
soothe them, taking all the time in the world.

They should, however, be given no ground for hope for any
reward other than to emerge alive. As the London police put it
at Spaghetti House and Balcombe Street when the kidnappers
demanded to be flown out of the country, 'there are only two
places you can go—to a cell or to a mortuary.' They should
constantly be reminded that, if the victim is harmed, the police
will attack without restraint. The only incentives are negative
ones. The longer or more violently they resist, the longer their
sentence is likely to be, and the likelier they are to die.

The negotiator should be a police officer who, though trained
and experienced in kidnap negotiations, is of fairly junior rank:
first, because he is likely to be better able to establish a relationship with the kidnappers; and second, because he must (like any
other negotiator) be able to say: 'I have no power to agree to that.
I'll have to ask.' On occasions, close friends or relatives have been
used to try to persuade the kidnappers to surrender but this can
be counterproductive, because it arouses their emotions and
increases the danger of them acting irrationally.

The kidnappers may try to push the hostage into acting as negotiator for his own release. This should not be accepted; first, because he is not a free agent; and second, because this will deny the police and their psychiatric adviser some of their opportunity to assess the kidnappers' state of mind.

The negotiator should, while constantly urging surrender, give nothing away too easily. The kidnappers must not be given food or water until their need is becoming desperate. Gradually they must be driven into the same situation which they had with their victim: that of a baby totally dependent for everything upon its mother.

It may, on occasions, be wise to allow them to have a transistor radio so that they can listen to the news. This can have snags—as once it did in New York, when a local radio station telephoned all the neighbours until they found one whose window overlooked the hideout, and put his voice live on the radio as he described the policemen creeping up on the building for an assault. More often, however, it may have a soothing effect, especially if the kidnappers have a political motive, and realize that their cause is receiving publicity. Also, if the police have established a good working relationship with all the radio stations, they may agree (with a life at stake) not to broadcast in such a way as to hamper the task of the police or increase the risk to the hostage. This was certainly done in the two London sieges.

During the siege, the rapport between the kidnappers and the hostage may increase. They will all perceive that the greatest threat to their lives now comes from the police. At Stockholm, the hostages came out screaming abuse at the police and one—at least—continued to visit her captor in prison for some time afterwards. This rapport must be understood for what it is by the police. The hostage has been undergoing an intense psychological strain, and should not be blamed. They should regard the rapport as an asset, and make full use of it.

At the same time, a good negotiator may gradually be able to build up a kind of rapport of his own with the kidnappers—especially if the impression is given that higher authority is being hard-nosed. The negotiator can exploit the 'mother and baby' relationship to the full.

The police should try to wear out the resistance of the kidnappers. Negotiators should work in shifts. Lights should constantly be beamed through the windows. Noise should keep them awake—one New York hostage team drove a truck up and down ceaselessly broadcasting a very loud tape calling on them to surrender.

The police psychiatric adviser should, if possible, be at the negotiator's side throughout. A microphone should, of course, be inserted as quickly as practicable (preferably without the kidnappers knowing it). All their conversation—with each other, or the hostage or the negotiator—should be taped; from the tapes the psychiatrist can judge how they are likely to react to new negotiating ploys, or to an assault. At the Stockholm siege, for example, the psychiatrist, Dr Bejerot, recommended the moment to release teargas into the locked bank vault. The doctors said that serious lung damage would result to the kidnappers and the hostages if they were not out within ninety seconds. The psychiatrist, armed with his continuous analysis of their conversation, staked his reputation on their opening the door more quickly than this, without harming themselves or their hostages—and he was right.

RAIDS

Most protracted sieges end with a surrender rather than a raid—though there are exceptions, such as the raid by the Dutch marines at Scheveningen, and then again in the second train and school hijacking in 1977, and at Assen in 1978 (see Chapter Thirteen). In both cases, they picked their time as a result of careful analysis of the kidnappers' conversation by psychiatrists. Dr Dik Mulder has, as a result, acquired a unique reputation in this field.

More often, raids are mounted to snatch the kidnappers and their hostage by surprise. This was attempted, unsuccessfully, when the Irish police discovered the hideout where Dr Herrema was being held at Monasterevin; after it failed, the eighteen-day siege began.

Successful raids in recent years include three on hijacked aircraft on the ground: by the Israelis at Lod in 1972, by the Israelis again at Entebbe in 1976, and by the Germans at Mogadishu in 1977.

The essence is the momentary confusion of the kidnappers by surprise and shock. This was achieved with 'stun grenades' at Mogadishu, where two members of the British Special Air Service (SAS) assisted. These grenades have the effect of stunning both kidnappers and hostages for a few vital seconds, without injuring them. The SAS are specially trained for raids of this type; and a number of other countries now also have such teams in their armies or police. The Dutch marines at Assen, too, relied upon noise to stun and disorient the terrorists.

THE HOSTAGE AFTER HIS RELEASE

Whether he is released by ransom, siege or raid, the hostage is likely to be shattered, physically and mentally, and to be in need of urgent medical care. On the other hand, he may appear to be so filled with joy and relief that he gives a false impression of his true condition. It must be assumed that the hostage will have been badly scarred, and that this may only become apparent later.

Though it may be necessary to take him to somewhere other than his own home (to avoid his being besieged by the press) he should be surrounded as soon as possible by familiar people and things; obviously, his family; his favourite clothes, food, drink, pipe etc.; even little things like his own shaving kit can greatly assist his psychological adjustment. His doctor should naturally be there; and he may need to be reassured that all is well with his business and personal affairs, which may have been preying on his mind.

He may, conceivably, welcome the chance to speak to the press, to say things he has been longing to say. (If he is an executive of a firm, the firm should be asked for its agreement.) Any exposure of the victim to the press, however, must be carefully handled. Most reporters were themselves shocked and ashamed by the treatment given by some of their profession to Mrs Matthews just after her release in Balcombe Street. Bombarded by news-hungry reporters from all sides, with flashlights popping and microphones thrust into her face, she looked like a hunted animal, and it was an inexcusable blunder to have subjected her to this without a much tighter degree of control—if at all—in the state in which she was. Others, however, have made a dignified and moving impression on the whole world, doing immense good for the community and to themselves, and underlining the contrast between their own courage and their kidnappers' cruelty and hypocrisy. The decision must depend on the state of the victim and the ordeal must be strictly limited in duration.

Much more important than press conferences is the victim's debriefing. This may make a decisive difference to the prospects of arrest of the kidnappers and recovery of the ransom. He will probably be glad to co-operate—though there may still be a residue, even a strong one, of the rapport with his kidnappers and of hostility towards the police. If so, this must be accepted with tact and understanding. His doctor must advise on the timing and extent of his debriefing.

Thereafter, for the weeks or months of recovery, he must be given complete privacy and security, amongst only his family and closest friends. Some people believe that he should be discouraged from talking or thinking about his ordeal but they are probably wrong. He may well feel a need to tell the whole story, and get it out of his system.

Later on, the kidnap victim often experiences severe psychological problems. First is a feeling of self-reproach, of guilt for being caught, for failing to make a heroic escape, for failing to resist interrogation, and for having caused a great deal of trouble to his family, his firm, his government and (if an expatriate) to his host government; he may also feel intensely guilty over the price that his family or firm have had to pay for his life. And he may fear that he is irreparably damaged in their eyes; that his firm will never regard him as fit to withstand heavy responsibility again; that the humiliation he suffered has degraded him for ever; even that he is regarded as 'a social pariah or a leper'.[1] On the other hand, he may later feel resentful that not enough was done to get him released, and that even his family does not appreciate what he went through. Several marriages

1. These are the precise words used by ex-hostages, as quoted by Brian Jenkins in his *Hostage Survival; Some Preliminary Observations* (Rand Corporation, Santa Monica, 1976).

have been broken by kidnapping, by the attitude of either the victim or his wife, or of both. He will need special understanding —perhaps for the rest of his life. He will need desperately to recover his pride, even if he gives an outward impression of confidence, or of regarding the whole experience as a joke.

Being kidnapped is what psychiatrists describe as a 'primary experience'—that is, one which threatens one's life. The humiliation of having been like a helpless infant, in the hands of people who may be criminals or physically repulsive student revolutionaries, is a traumatic experience. The victim may indeed dream about it, have periods of melancholia, and be jumpy with strangers, unpredictably, for ever.

Great as the strains may be upon the firm, the negotiators and the police, they should remind themselves that the greatest strain of all falls upon the victim and his family. Because of its open-endedness and uncertainty, being kidnapped is far worse than serving a prison sentence, and one of the worst and most prolonged forms of torture that any human being can inflict upon another. The inspiring conclusion from studying this cruelty is man's ability to survive it.

III. CASE STUDIES

Chapter Eleven

Great Britain

MRS MURIEL MACKAY

KIDNAPPING was almost unknown in Britain until 1969 and, although there have still been very few, the cases which have occurred have taught some valuable lessons, particularly about police co-operation with families and with the media.

Mrs Muriel Mackay, wife of a senior newspaperman, was taken by two criminal kidnappers from her home in Wimbledon in 1969. It later transpired that they had taken the wrong person, and had intended to kidnap the wife of the newspaper millionnaire Rupert Murdoch. They telephoned a demand for £1 million ($1,800,000) to Scotland Yard. The kidnappers, two brothers from Trinidad, were traced and later convicted through the use of an identifiable car at a ransom rendezvous; but Mrs Mackay had already been murdered, and her body was never found.

The police investigation was conducted in a glare of publicity. Telephone lines were blocked, and detectives and relatives were relentlessly followed by journalists. Sir Robert Mark considered that this almost certainly ensured the death of the victim; and the débâcle prompted the Metropolitan Police to launch a serious study of the handling of kidnapping.

LESLEY WHITTLE

There were thereafter no more serious kidnappings in Britain until 1975—though there are always a few local abductions within families or local communities. Early in 1975, however, the first of a series of cases occurred in the Midlands. Lesley Whittle, aged seventeen, had been left £82,000 ($150,000) in trust by her father, who had died four years earlier. Some controversy about the will had been published in the press; and this was picked up by a dangerous criminal, Donald Neilson, who thereafter began a long and careful preparation for a kidnap and ransom.

Lesley lived with her mother and her brother Ronald in a village in Shropshire. On 14th January 1975 Neilson, armed and hooded, broke silently into her bedroom and took her out at gunpoint. After putting the terrified girl in his car, he went back into the house and left a prepared ransom demand stamped on red embossing tape in the living room. This demanded £50,000 ($90,000) in £1 and £5 notes, and gave orders to await instructions at a particular telephone box; it also warned that, if the police were informed, Lesley would be killed.

Ronald Whittle did inform the police and two days later, with their full co-operation, followed written instructions which the kidnapper had left behind the backboard in a telephone box, and went on to a 2 a.m. rendezvous in Bathpool Park near Kidsgrove, about sixty miles from his home. He had the ransom money with him in a suitcase, but lost his way and arrived late.

The police had seen these instructions, and had established full surveillance at the Bathpool Park rendezvous. Unfortunately, however, there was a lack of co-ordination. Britain has fifty-one police forces, and three of them were involved: West Mercia, whose area included the Whittle's home; Staffordshire, whose area included Bathpool Park; and the Metropolitan Police, who had sent up a team of Scotland Yard detectives at the request of the West Mercia Police.

Twelve Scotland Yard cars were deployed in Bathpool Park when, to their horror—and before Ronald Whittle had arrived with the ransom money—a Staffordshire police car, with flashing lights, drove in and started checking the numbers of all the cars in the area, including the Scotland Yard cars.

Neilson, who was watching, naturally shied off and took cover in the underground drainage system in the park, around which he had built up his plan—and in which Lesley Whittle was being held prisoner. He had placed her on the platform of a drainage shaft, fifty feet below ground, restrained by a steel wire secured round her neck. While her brother was vainly trying to keep the rendezvous above, with Scotland Yard men all around, Neilson returned, thoroughly alarmed, to this platform. Lesley Whittle then fell off it (he said accidentally, though the prosecution argued that he had killed her to get rid of the evidence) and was hanged by the steel wire.

The officer in charge of the case, Chief Superintendent Booth of the West Mercia Police, did not, of course, know that Lesley Whittle was dead, but he did realize that the blunder over the surveillance would have caused Neilson to suspect police involvement (though, ironically, the Staffordshire police car had nothing to do with the operation). Booth and Ronald Whittle, therefore, made somewhat desperate efforts to put up a smoke-screen suggesting that, though they had been in contact, they had now fallen out. Ten days after the abortive rendezvous, Chief Superintendent Booth, in a television interview, suggested that 'a member of the family has had some communication and has not seen fit—only in the interests of the child—to tell us.' Next day, Ronald was interviewed, and said: 'The chances of getting Lesley back alive must be improved if the police are kept out of it . . . there has been a conflict of priorities. They want to capture the kidnappers. I want Lesley back safely.'

Various other attempts were made, by both Booth and Ronald Whittle, to give the impression of a breach, in an elaborate television charade over the next few weeks.

Lesley Whittle's body was found on 7th March, naked and still hanging by the steel rope, in the drainage shaft. The suffering and terror which she must have endured before she died are almost too horrifying to bear thinking about. Neilson, who had operated on his own, was arrested in December 1975 and sentenced to life imprisonment for this crime, and for several other murders.

This ghastly case illustrates, above all, two things: first, that the loner may be more dangerous to the victim than the well organized professional gang; and second, that if the police do try to monitor the delivery of the ransom, it must be regarded as an intensely delicate operation, requiring the most careful co-ordination. Any bungling is likely, as on this occasion, to prove fatal.

ALIO KALOGHIROU

On 6th November 1975—eight months after Lesley Whittle's
body had been found, but before her kidnapper was arrested—
an eighteen-year-old Cypriot girl, Alio Kaloghirou, was kidnapped from her home in London by two men wearing stocking
masks. A ransom demand for £60,000 ($110,000) was left on the
table, with the usual warning not to tell the police.

The family did tell the police; but thereafter both maintained
the utmost discretion. Scotland Yard took representatives of
twenty London papers, radio and television authorities fully into
their confidence, and briefed them every day for nine days; they
were told that, if any of them leaked the story, it would probably
result in the death of the girl. None wished to risk being blamed
for doing this, and all were confident that the others would not
either; so all of them voluntarily kept quiet.

Meanwhile, telephone negotiations proceeded between the
kidnappers and the girl's family. These were taped, and the
police kept informed. The kidnappers eventually agreed to accept
£17,000 ($31,000); and her brother-in-law was instructed to
leave it, in used £5 and £10 notes, in a builder's skip near Bounds
Green railway station. This was done; and in the early hours of
the morning she was dumped by the roadside, blindfolded, not
far away. Three hours later, all the kidnap gang (five men) were
arrested, and the money recovered.

The police had deployed over 100 detectives on a full but
discreet surveillance of the entire operation. They had, however,
earned and retained the full co-operation both of the family and
of the media.

The Times praised the police, and justified their decision to
ask them and other papers not to report the case. They summed
up the dilemma succinctly as follows:[1]

> For any particular family the safety of the victim is the overriding
> concern; but nothing would be more likely to make kidnapping a
> common crime in Britain than a series of private bargains between

1. *The Times*, 17th November 1975.

criminals and families afraid to go to the police. The motives of the police cannot be identical with those of the family, for they must give more weight to the public interest in making crime unrewarding. But they are hampered in that aim if they cannot convince a victim's family that they are willing to make his or her safety their most immediate concern and able to give credible assurances that it will not be jeopardized by inopportune publicity.

SPAGHETTI HOUSE AND BALCOMBE STREET

In two other kidnappings in London at about the same time, the Metropolitan Police again demonstrated the skill which they had acquired in co-operating with a free press—though in neither of these cases was secrecy either possible or requested.

In September 1975, three armed criminals seized six hostages in the basement of the Spaghetti House Restaurant after an attempt at armed robbery had been foiled. The police took the media into their confidence, and told the BBC and local radio stations, in particular, that they had given the kidnappers a radio in exchange for the release of a sick hostage. The radio stations co-operated by voluntarily editing their broadcasts so as not to hamper the police or place the hostages at risk. Aided by a psychiatrist, the police wore down the kidnappers, who were arrested, and all the hostages released unharmed, after six days.

The Balcombe Street siege began on 6th December 1975, in a different way but it was similarly handled. A gang of four IRA men made an armed attack on a restaurant in the West End of London. The police had detected a pattern in the raids by this gang, and had deployed a wide network of armed police in the area. A gun battle ensued; and the gang took refuge in a flat in Balcombe Street, holding its occupants, Mr and Mrs Matthews, as hostages. The shooting had ruled out any question of secrecy, so again the police took great trouble to brief the press. On the sixth day of the siege, a huge cloth screen was erected to block the cameras for what was expected—and, in fact, proved—to be the final stage. At the same time, the arrival of the army's special assault team from the SAS was calculatedly leaked to the press and the BBC. Very soon afterwards the kidnappers surrendered, having first released the hostages unharmed. The actual release was a dramatic scene, with the two hostages, obviously exhausted, emerging with hands raised on to the balcony to walk to the next flat, under cover of police marksmen in the foreground. This was filmed, under close police control, and broadcast worldwide on television that evening.

Thus, after a disastrous start with Lesley Whittle in January (though this was not in London), the police had, by the end of 1975, developed a high degree of skill in co-operating both with families and with the media in kidnapping situations, and in handling sieges. They emerged as a result with a greatly enhanced reputation with the public; and this was reflected in public co-operation, not only over kidnapping, but in many other ways. Up to the time of writing (summer 1978) there have been no more serious kidnappings, either for ransom or for political blackmail, in Great Britain.

Chapter Twelve

Ireland—North and South

NORTHERN IRELAND

CONSIDERING the scale of violence in Northern Ireland since 1971, there has been remarkably little kidnapping. One reason for this may be that most of the hardcore members of the Provisional IRA (which has probably varied from 700 at its peak to about 200 in 1978) are known to the police, though they cannot be arrested unless there is evidence of a crime. If, therefore, they were to attempt to hold a hostage for any length of time, there would be a strong likelihood of the hideout being found.

Much more common, therefore, has been assassination. Although most of the 1,350 civilians killed in Northern Ireland have been victims of indiscriminate bombings, about 450 of them have been killed in individual or sectarian murders. Some of these have first been kidnapped but this has merely been to take them away to some quiet spot where they can be murdered in secret. Others have been picked up in the same way for knee-capping or lesser punishments. Few have been held for more than a few hours. Under the threat of assassination, however, there have been some cases of extortion of protection money, ranging from £2,800 reputedly paid by the Anglo-Irish Bank in 1977, through £400 per week paid by some hotels as an alternative to being bombed, down to £1 per day by taxi drivers as the price of plying for hire in certain areas.

One bank employee was kidnapped in Belfast for a ransom of £25,000 ($45,000) but the gang was arrested almost at once. This was probably intended more as a form of bank robbery than as a kidnapping. Otherwise there have been no reported cases of kidnapping for ransom or for political coercion of the government.

The only kidnapping of the more typical kind was that of the West German consul, Thomas Niedermayer, who was taken from his Belfast home in January 1974, and has never been heard of since; nor has any demand, either for a ransom or for political concessions, been received.

DR TIEDE HERREMA

The only victim in recent years of a straightforward kidnapping in the Republic of Ireland has been Dr Tiede Herrema, manager of the Dutch-owned Ferenko steel plant in Limerick. He was driving in his car on the way to work on 3rd October 1975 when he was flagged down by a Provisional IRA man, Eddie Gallagher, who was dressed as a policeman. Having asked him his name, Gallagher pulled out a pistol and kidnapped him. He was taken first to a deserted farmhouse for a week; then, for another week, held in a second house; and finally transferred to a council house in Monastarevin.

Gallagher, aged twenty-seven, was accompanied throughout by a twenty-one-year-old girl, Marion Coyle. There were probably only three or four others concerned, chiefly the normal occupants of the safe houses. Only Gallagher and Coyle were involved in guarding Dr Herrema. Their operation was disowned by the IRA army council, who had earlier accused Gallagher of embezzling £90,000 ($160,000) from the proceeds of bank robberies on their behalf.

On the first day, from the farmhouse, they issued a demand for the release of three prisoners held in the Republic: Dr Rose Dugdale, an English IRA supporter by whom Gallagher had already conceived a child; and Kevin Mallon and Jim Hyland, one of whom was believed to be Marion Coyle's boyfriend. Unless this was done within forty-eight hours, they said, Dr Herrema would be killed.

The Irish government refused the demand, and named Gallagher and Coyle as wanted for the crime. They appointed a mediator, Father O'Mahoney, who made contact through an intermediary with the kidnappers on 8th October.

For the first five days, in the farmhouse, Dr Herrema was kept blindfolded, with his ears plugged, and without food. On 15th October, the Irish government received a tape of his voice, in which he said that the kidnappers had threatened to cut off his foot and send it to the government if they demanded proof that he was alive.

On 20th October the Irish police found the car used by Gallagher, and arrested two men accused of being accomplices. They searched the house in Monastarevin; but the kidnappers managed to escape detection in the attic. On 21st October the police again surrounded the house, and this time trapped the kidnappers in an upstairs bedroom. They fired when police tried to mount the stairs, and threatened to kill Dr Herrema if they tried again.

Then began an eighteen-day siege. The police kept the kidnappers awake by constant noise, and by floodlights trained on their window. For the first four days Dr Herrema had no food and, presumably, Gallagher and Coyle had very little either. They thereafter accepted food, and a chamber pot for sanitation. Dr Herrema, whose feet were tied throughout the siege, was forced from time to time to stand at the window at gunpoint, and shout to the police not to come near.

The bedroom was quickly bugged by the police, and miniature television cameras were installed. Scotland Yard sent over officers who had been involved in the Spaghetti House siege to help and advise. The Irish police offered no concessions. They worked in shifts to maintain a continuous argument which, along with the light and the noise, was designed to wear the kidnappers down.

On the tenth day of the siege, two police officers, hoping that the kidnappers were losing their alertness, climbed a ladder to try to get in through the upstairs lavatory window. Gallagher, however, spotted them and fired, wounding one of them in the hand.

By 7th November, Gallagher was becoming exhausted, with severe stomach pains, and was persuaded to release Dr Herrema and surrender.

Despite Gallagher's periodic fits of violence, Dr Herrema had managed to build up at least a *modus vivendi*, with some conversation about Gallagher's relationship with Rose Dugdale. Just before he surrendered, Gallagher gave Dr Herrema a bullet from his gun as a souvenir.

Gallagher's behaviour was that of a violent criminal, rather than of a political terrorist. In the end, he showed at least a spark of human feeling. Not so Marion Coyle, in whom no vestige of humanity seems to have survived. Spending five weeks within a few feet of Dr Herrema, under intense stress, she never said a single word to him nor answered a single word he said to her. He was not even one of the 'enemy'—the English—but simply a representative of capitalism (she and Gallagher claimed to be members of a revolutionary organization far bigger than the IRA). Her behaviour and attitude—matched only by that of members of the Japanese Red Army—is an awe-inspiring example of what political indoctrination can do to the human spirit.

Chapter Thirteen

The Netherlands

THE HAGUE

THE Dutch government has one of the best records in the world for handling kidnapping and hostage situations. They have been pioneers: both in training a special assault force for the release of hostages; and in the co-operation between this force and their psychiatric adviser in planning and timing the assault.

The Special Aid Unit (BBE) of Dutch marines was formed, like the German GSG9 squad described in the next chapter, after the kidnapping and murder of the Olympic athletes at Munich in 1972; it was used with great success at Scheveningen in 1974, then in the second train hijacking in 1977, and again at Assen in 1978. These incidents are described later in this chapter.

The first major political kidnapping in Holland was, however, of a very different kind, and, though the marines stood by, they were not used. This took place in the Hague on 13th September 1974, and provides remarkable illustration of the international terrorist network in action—its members, including the Japanese Red Army, the German RAF, the PFLP and Carlos; and its extent, through Germany, Switzerland, Holland and France.

In July 1974, the French arrested a Japanese courier, Yoshiaki Yamada, who was attempting to smuggle 10,000 counterfeit dollars into France to finance an operation to kidnap two Japanese businessmen in Germany. A few weeks later, a plan was put in motion to perform another kidnapping to force the release of Yamada, involving Carlos and Moukharbel, the PFLP courier whom he was later to kill (see Chapter Three). On 3rd September, Carlos and Moukharbel went to Zurich, where they met three JRA terrorists to whom they delivered money and weapons, including some grenades stolen in 1971 by the Baader-Meinhof group from a US army base in Germany.

On 12th September, Carlos accompanied these three Japanese to Amsterdam; and next day (without Carlos), they seized the French embassy in the Hague, holding the French ambassador and ten other hostages. They demanded that the French should release Yamada to join them, and that they should all be flown to the Middle East with a ransom of a million dollars. They said they would kill the hostages one by one at intervals until this demand was granted.

The French did release Yamada and the four were flown to Damascus with $300,000. The Syrians confiscated the ransom, but allowed the four terrorists to go on to rejoin the JRA base with the PFLP in Lebanon.

SCHEVENINGEN

On 26th October 1974, four convicts at Scheveningen Prison, who had managed to acquire two pistols, seized fifteen hostages in the prison chapel during mass. Two of the convicts were Dutch and two were Arabs; they demanded a plane to fly them to an Arab country. The Dutch authorities had inserted a microphone, and started on the business of wearing down the kidnappers with the advice of a psychiatrist. Early in the morning of the fifth day, they used a thermal lance to burn through the lock; then fifteen Dutch marines burst into the chapel, making as much noise as possible. The kidnappers, who were nearing exhaustion, were taken by surprise. They were arrested, and all the hostages were freed without anyone being hurt.

THE FIRST TRAIN HIJACK

On Tuesday 2nd December 1975, six South Moluccans hijacked a train near Beilen and held about fifty passengers as hostages. Their aim was to publicize their claim for the independence of their islands from Indonesia, over which they felt that the Dutch had let them down. Their more immediate demand was for a bus to take them and their hostages to an airport, to be flown to an unnamed destination.

They were remarkably vicious. Soon after the hijack, they shot the train driver dead. A few hours later, they shot another passenger in cold blood in the door of the train—as a demonstration of intent to the Dutch police watching from a distance. They threw the two bodies out of the train that afternoon. Two days later they shot a third hostage.

On 4th December, seven more South Moluccans seized the Indonesian consulate in Amsterdam, holding thirty-two hostages including seventeen children (there was a school in the consulate).

Eventually all the kidnappers surrendered: those in the train on 14th December and those in the consulate on 19th December.

The surrender of the train hijackers was particularly interesting. One of the hostages, Hans Prinz, had emerged as the spokesman for their discussions with the hijackers. Towards the end of the siege, he realized that they were getting desperate because no one was taking any notice of their demands. No bus had appeared and, after twelve days, they had no idea what was going on outside. He had developed some degree of rapport with them and they had by then permitted some of the hostages to leave: the aged, the sick, and a pregnant woman. But Prinz feared that, in their desperation, they were becoming unstable, and might soon start shooting hostages again. He therefore asked the police to send in a portable radio (there was none on the train). As they listened, the terrorists realized that everyone in Holland was talking and thinking about little else but the two South Moluccan sieges. After a few hours, they surrendered, their primary aim achieved.

One is reminded of Mohammed Ali's remarks after his world heavyweight championship fight in Zaïre: 'I never heard of Zaïre before I fought there. *Nobody* ever heard of Zaïre before I fought there. Now everybody's heard of Zaïre!'

Before the Beilen train hijacking, few people had ever heard of the South Moluccans. Now everybody has heard of the South Moluccans.

Publicity, however, was all they achieved, and it did not seem to advance their cause. There was no way in which the Dutch could force the Indonesians to give the islands their independence and the sympathy which many Dutchmen had felt for them was largely thrown away. The subsequent hijackings did nothing to restore their sympathy.

THE SECOND TRAIN HIJACK

On the morning of 23rd May 1977 two days before the Dutch general election nine South Moluccans hijacked a train near Glimmen, and another five seized a school at Bovensmilde.

The school lies in a mixed Dutch and South Moluccan housing estate. Its seizure appears to have been a private venture by South Moluccans from the neighbouring houses, who were frustrated by not being selected to take part in the train hijacking. They held 125 white children aged between six and twelve, with five teachers, having released the twenty South Moluccan children they found there. Three days later, an epidemic of vomiting and diarrhoea broke out (the authorities denied having doctored the food they sent in), and all the children were released. One of the teachers also became ill and was released next day; and at some stage one of the kidnappers got away to the South Moluccan houses which backed on to the school, leaving four terrorists and four hostages inside. The school was, of course, surrounded by the police. They were somewhat hampered by reporters, who were offering large sums to householders for the use of rooms overlooking the school.

Meanwhile the nine terrorists on the train had released a number of old and young passengers and held fifty-five hostages. Their demands included the release of twenty-one South Moluccans held in prison for various terrorist offences, including those convicted for the Beilen train hijacking; they demanded buses to take them and their hostages to Amsterdam airport, from which they, the released terrorists and all the hostages were to be flown to an unnamed destination.

They gave a deadline of 2 p.m. on 24th May (that is, about twenty-nine hours after the hijacking), but the Dutch government refused to negotiate in any way until all the children had been released from the school. The train hijackers appear to have been taken by surprise by the school hijacking, and the deadline passed without incident. On the third day (before the release of the schoolchildren), the train hijackers attempted to put pressure on the authorities by parading three of the hostages outside the train with ropes round their necks but there was again no reaction and after a time the hostages were taken back into the train.

Two Moluccan mediators, accepted by both sides, went on board the train. The terrorists' demands remained unchanged, though with no deadline.

Meanwhile, the Dutch government was determined not to release the convicted terrorists—especially those who had murdered the three hostages at Beilen. The marines had managed to insert listening devices along the whole length of the train during darkness, and the psychiatrist (Dr Dik Mulder) and the marine assault force began to build up a picture of where the terrorists and the hostages were located in the train, and of their relationship and state of mind. They were helped in this by two pregnant women who were released on 5th June.

It was decided to assault the train and the school to rescue the hostages simultaneously at dawn (4.53 a.m.) on the nineteenth day of the siege, 11th June.

Little resistance was anticipated in the school. Four armoured troop-carriers breached the walls of the school buildings and pulled back a few feet to allow the marines to debouch and charge through the gaps. Kidnappers and hostages all appeared to be paralyzed with fright and no one was hurt.

The assault on the train was very different. The marines knew that the terrorists were led by a fanatic; that all of them had probably received military training in the Dutch army; that the hostages were all held in two coaches of the train (men in one, women in the other), with the terrorists normally sleeping in two groups, one at the front of the train and the other behind the hostages. They also knew that the hostage compartments were only lightly guarded at night, if at all, and that the terrorists were at their lowest ebb in the early hours of the morning.

During the night, the marines placed a number of small charges with electrically controlled detonators at various points beside the train. At dawn, these charges were set off, and six fighter aircraft flew low over the train. Simultaneously, marksmen with machine guns poured covering fire into the two compartments where the terrorists were known to sleep. Under the cover of this fire and confusion, the marines' assault force advanced to the train behind smoke grenades and blasted their way in with prepared charges.

All the time, loudhailers were warning the hostages to remain lying down. While one of the kidnappers was exchanging fire with a marine inside the train, one of the hostages stood up and was killed (bullets from both sides were found in his body). Another, a girl, was killed by terrorist bullets, apparently whilst trying to move from one compartment to another. Two marines and five other hostages were wounded. Six of the terrorists were killed, and one severely wounded. The other two had taken no part in resisting the attack, and were picked up, frightened but unhurt, hiding under blankets with the women hostages. The whole operation had taken twenty-two minutes.

Assen

On Monday 13th March 1978, three armed South Moluccan terrorists broke into the local government offices in Assen. Most of the staff escaped, but seventy-two were held hostage. The terrorists shot one of them and threw him out of the window. It was uncertain whether he was dead, so a military armoured car drove up to try to pick him up. The terrorists placed another hostage at a window, and said that he too would be shot if the armoured car picked up the other one.

The terrorists demanded the release of twenty-one South Moluccans from prison (including those convicted for the previous sieges.) They demanded that the released prisoners, fifty of the hostages and the three terrorists themselves should be taken by bus to the airport to be flown to an unnamed destination—with a ransom of $12 million.

The Dutch government refused but next day sent in two Moluccan mediators, who had no success, but brought out a message that the terrorists would start killing hostages unless their demands were granted. They would shoot two hostages at 2 p.m. (14th March) and continue to shoot two more every half-hour thereafter.

The Dutch government felt that there was a risk that this threat would be carried out, so they decided to send in the marines. There was little time for planning but they were helped by a woman hostage who had been released with the mediators, and who was able to tell them how many terrorists there were, and where people were located in the building.

Soon after 2 p.m. the terrorists selected the first two hostages for shooting—two local government deputies—and placed them on chairs ready to be shot. At 2.43 p.m. the marines went in and, after a few minutes, captured all three terrorists unhurt. Four of the hostages in the building were injured. The man who had been thrown out of the window was dead.

The effect of all these sieges on the bulk of the South Moluccans in Holland has been tragic. The reason why they came to Holland at all was that they feared retribution from the Indonesians for remaining loyal to the Dutch during the war of independence—and earlier, during the Japanese occupation. Now, because of the violence of a few of them, the word 'South Moluccan' had become associated with savagery and cruelty— just as the bulk of Palestinians have been saddled with that image by a few hundred in the PFLP. The cold-blooded murder of the three hostages in the first train siege at Beilen, the kidnapping of young schoolchildren at Bovensmilde (not far from Assen) and now the callous refusal to allow the dead or dying man to be picked up outside the window, had aroused disgust all over the world—but especially in Holland, the land where the South Moluccans now have no option but to live, and whose inhabitants are their best (and almost their only) friends.

Chapter Fourteen

France

BARON EMPAIN

BARON EMPAIN, a forty-one-year-old Belgian multimillionaire, was kidnapped outside his flat in Paris on 23rd January 1978. He had left instructions that no ransom was to be paid, and his wife initially respected this; but on the third day the kidnappers cut off the little finger of his left hand and sent it to her. The Baron was held for sixty-three days in three hideouts, the last one being in a tent in the cellar of a suburban house in Paris, chained hand and foot and usually hooded. He lost two stone in weight during his confinement.

The family, however, co-operated with the police throughout and there was a virtual news blackout after the initial reports of the kidnapping. The initial demand was for a ransom of $20 million. After two months of negotiation the family agreed to pay $8 million. By then, the police were ready to act and the man who delivered the ransom was in fact a police inspector. On 23rd March, he went through the usual treasure hunt of clues but the kidnappers made no contact, presumably just satisfying themselves that there was no police surveillance. The police were discreet enough not to be spotted and next day (Good Friday) they ambushed the drop, killing one kidnapper and capturing another. Three men escaped.

The captured kidnapper was thirty-nine-year-old Alain Caillol, who was a leader—if not the leader—of the gang. Son of a successful manufacturer, he lived in a luxurious villa with a swimming pool, managing a branch of the firm, but leading a double life as a criminal.

The French have the death penalty for kidnapping and murder; and Caillol realized that, if the Baron were killed, he would be

guillotined. He therefore telephoned the rest of the gang from
the police inspector's office, and warned them that their only
hope of themselves escaping the guillotine was to release the
Baron at once. The Baron was dumped on Easter Sunday (26th
March) in the outskirts of Paris, and travelled seventeen stations
on the Métro to the centre of the city before telephoning his wife
to pick him up. The police located the final hideout, and further
arrests were made.

This case illustrates many of the seeds of success in dealing
with a criminal kidnapping: the victim's family, who could well
afford a large ransom, were patient, and co-operated with the
police; the police allowed them latitude in negotiation, and
showed admirable discretion and skill in ambushing the drop;
and the handling of the case after the ambush led to the recovery
of the victim alive, without payment of a ransom. This was also
a case in which the existence of the death penalty strengthened
the hand of the police.

Chapter Fifteen

West Germany

HANNS-MARTIN SCHLEYER

THE origins and motivation of the Red Army Fraction were described in Chapter One. To recapitulate briefly, they were a symptom not of Germany's shortcomings, but of her success. Born of student disaffection in 1968, the RAF members were frustrated by their inability either to influence the stable political system, or to get any support from the growingly prosperous proletariat whom they wanted to lead. After the first and second generations had been broken up in 1972 and 1975–6, a third, more ruthless and more professional generation of terrorists emerged in April 1977, self-contained and scorning the support of the idealistic students who had sympathized with their predecessors. To show their hatred and contempt for the state, they chose as their victims well guarded public figures such as the public prosecutor, Siegfried Buback, and the chairman of the Dresdner Bank, Jürgen Ponto; and then, in September 1977 the president of the Employers' and Industrial Associations, Dr Hanns-Martin Schleyer.

Schleyer's name was one of sixty on the coded RAF list found by the German police in November 1976. He himself had no doubts about the threat. At the memorial service to Jürgen Ponto, he remarked to a friend that 'the next victim of terrorism is almost certainly standing in this room now.'

He was therefore provided with three police guards and an escort car. The kidnapping took place at 5.30 p.m. on Monday 5th September 1977, in a one-way street close to his home. As they came round a corner, a white Volkswagen minibus blocked the road, and a girl terrorist pushed a pram off the pavement into the path of Schleyer's car—which was, surprisingly, not fitted

with the kind of security features which might have been expected for a man sufficiently under threat to justify a special
police guard. Another car (a yellow Mercedes) approached head
on, going the wrong way down the one-way street. The driver of
Schleyer's car, rather than run into the pram, braked so hard
that the escort vehicle ran into its back. About five terrorists
emerged from the minibus and from behind, and fired about 100
rounds in ninety seconds to kill the driver and all the bodyguards;
but skilfully avoided damaging their potential trump card,
Schleyer himself.

It is now possible to piece together the movements of the gang
and their hostage for the first three weeks after the kidnap. These
teach a number of important lessons. Papers captured when
Siegfried Haag was arrested in November 1976 contained details
(in code) which may have been for this kidnap or for kidnapping
generally. These included an instruction to establish several
alternative hideouts within one or two kilometres of the kidnap
site (though most were, in the event, a good deal further away).
The police found the place from which the operation was mounted, and also the first two hideouts—but both just too late.
Ironically, one of the causes of their missing the second one arose
from the extent of the public desire to help the police: there was
such a flood of information that no particular significance was
attached to one report from the occupants of a neighbouring flat
which in fact contained the vital clue, and no action was taken on
it.

The kidnap was mounted from a block of flats with a basement
car park in Wiener Weg 1, in Cologne—about three kilometres
from the spot where Schleyer was taken. Flat 2065 and parking
space 127 had been rented by a girl using the name of Lisa Ries,
about six weeks before the kidnap. She was in fact Friederike
Krabbe, sister of one of the terrorists imprisoned after the
Stockholm siege (and amongst the eleven whose release was
demanded for Schleyer's life). A man pretending to be Lisa
Ries's fiancé', who had some dealings with the caretaker over the
parking of vehicles in space 127, was Willy Peter Stoll, also on the
wanted list. The caretaker was able to describe them both, and
he had also noted the number of the white Volkswagen minibus
and the yellow Mercedes, which had regularly been parked there.

The caretaker, hearing the radio news of the kidnapping, informed the police; they found the minibus back in space 127 at 8 p.m. and searched flat 2065 but it was, of course, empty. The kidnappers may have intended this, as the first kidnap message was waiting for the police in the minibus.

The kidnappers probably transferred Schleyer from the minibus to another vehicle for delivery to what is now believed to have been his first hideout, the University Centre, or Uni Zenter, a huge, forty-three-storey block of flats located not far away. This contained 960 flats, housing 2,500 people (including 650 students). Few of the occupants knew their often changing neighbours, and up to 100 flats might normally be expected to be empty. (On one occasion a man wanted by the police got hold of a key and occupied an empty flat on the thirty-seventh floor for several weeks; no one noticed until someone complained about his noisy radio.) Between five and ten flats changed hands every week and the occupants were by no means all Germans.

So there seemed nothing unusual about a girl of twenty-two who rented a flat on the twenty-sixth floor, producing normal evidence of identity and paying two months' rent in advance. This was on 15th August (three weeks before the kidnap). She used the name of Marquand but was in fact Adelheid Schulz, who was already on the wanted list on suspicion of complicity in the murder of Jürgen Ponto. She was given the key to her flat, together with a parking permit in the basement and a key giving access to the lift to take her direct from the basement to the twenty-sixth floor. Once in the lift, of course, she did not have to pass the desk of the concierge, as tenants or visitors on foot have to do.

A few days after the kidnapping, an Alfa-Romeo car was found in this basement; its registration linked it to one 'Konrad Binder' —known to be an alias used by Rolf Heissler, one of the original first-generation terrorists still at large, and wanted for an armed bank raid. Its parking place did not link it to the flat, but was one of hundreds amongst the maze of concrete pillars, nooks and crannies in the basement. The kidnappers are unlikely to have used the Alfa-Romeo to bring Schleyer in, or to have left it there if they had, so it was probably used only for access for gang members after the kidnap. Assuming that he was delivered in a van, it would have been very easy to take him up to the twenty-sixth floor in the lift, possibly rolled up in a carpet or locked in a box or wardrobe—nothing unusual about that, with so many moving in and out.

After identifying the car, the police discreetly guarded all exits, did a quick check with the block office and searched any flats about which there was any doubt. Meanwhile a couple of plain-clothes policemen rented a flat; and detailed plans were made both for a full search and, if the hideout were located, for a raid by the GSG9. The search took eight days—but the birds had flown even before the car was found.

They had, in fact, moved to a third-floor flat in a much smaller block in the quiet little dormitory town of Liblar, sixteen kilo-metres out of Cologne. Since this block was smaller and less impersonal, some of the neighbours *had* noticed that the third-floor flat had been taken and the rent paid in advance, but that no one had moved in. When the kidnapping occurred, this un-usual fact was reported to the police—one of a total of 3,826 such messages—but seemed of no great consequence. A day or two later some people did move in, with a box or cupboard—con-taining Schleyer. About two weeks later they moved out, again with one large piece of furniture, which was put into a van. That did seem a little odd, and was reported again. This time the report was acted upon—but by then the flat was empty.

It is uncertain where they went next: possibly across the Belgian or Dutch frontiers, scarcely an hour's run away, with many minor crossings and little control; there was a report of Schleyer being held for a time in a boat in a canal or an inland sea in Holland, and even a (false) conjecture that he might have been taken to England. His body was, in the event, found in France.

His own behaviour was staunch and courageous. He had left a letter with a friend saying that he wished the government to make no concessions to obtain his release. In his letters to his wife, written at gunpoint and censored by his kidnappers, he studiously avoided any words which might suggest that the government should give way. This also applied to two statements on film, which were later shown on television worldwide.

Meanwhile, the RAF's older intellectual sympathizers were

putting their case in France. One of their lawyers, Klaus Croissant, had crossed the frontier to escape arrest by the German police, and he spoke on French television in support of the RAF. A well known French playwright, Jean Genêt, was given a prominent space in *Le Monde* for an article expressing gratitude to Baader, Meinhof and the RAF, and saying that their violence was justified by the brutality of the system in West Germany, which he described as an American outpost against the Russians.

The first kidnap message had demanded the release of eleven RAF terrorists serving sentences in prison, including Baader, Ennslin, Hanna Krabbe and two others convicted for the hostage murders at Stockholm—but, surprisingly, not Siegfried Haag (who, it is reported, was much put out by this). These eleven were to be taken to an airport by 10 a.m. on Wednesday 7th September, to be flown to a country of their choice, each with $45,000; the kidnappers also demanded that their communication should be read out in full on television on the Tuesday evening (6th September). The government ignored both deadlines, and demanded proof that Schleyer was still alive.

The deadline was twice extended (to midday on 9th September and midnight on 12th September) but again ignored. Chancellor Schmidt warned the terrorists that they were fighting a losing battle, and imposed a news blackout. In view of the suspicion that there was contact between the kidnappers and their comrades in prison, he also suspended visits by their lawyers.

The German government, while maintaining an uncompromising line in its negotiations and public pronouncements, was meanwhile displaying considerable shrewdness in playing for time. There were periodic reports of German ministers flying for consultations to places such as Algeria, Libya, Iraq, South Yemen and Vietnam. While nothing was said about the purpose of these visits, the press predictably conjectured that they were examining the possibilities of those countries receiving the terrorists if they were released from prison. This probably encouraged the kidnappers not to kill Schleyer, so long as there seemed to be a chance of their demands being met.

MOGADISHU AND ITS CONSEQUENCES

On 13th October the drama took a new turn with the hijacking of a Lufthansa aircraft carrying seventy-nine passengers and a crew of five. The hijackers demanded the release of the same eleven RAF prisoners, with some additional demands, and it was at first assumed that they also were Germans.

They were, in fact, Arabs, and this hijacking again illustrates the remarkable links between the RAF and the Palestinians. The leader called himself 'Captain Mahmoud'—but he was later identified as Zuheir Youssef Okasha, who had recently slipped out of Britain, unnoticed, where he was wanted for the murder of the North Yemeni prime minister and two others in London on 9th April 1977. The passengers described him as unbalanced and unpredictable, and his rhetoric, both with them and in radio negotiations with airport control towers, was concerned with world revolution and was often hysterical. Yet there were indications of considerable organization behind him.

The hijackers had boarded the plane as passengers at Palma, Majorca, where they believed that security was slack. In what has now become the common fate of hijacked aircraft, it was turned away from a succession of Arab airports (Damascus, Baghdad and Kuwait) and permitted to refuel in Rome, Cyprus, Bahrain and (reluctantly) Dubai, where it remained for thirty hours. While negotiating over the radio about deadlines, the German government, in view of Mahmoud's instability, despatched a twenty-eight man team from its GSG9 assault force, initially to Cyprus and then to Dubai; but the aircraft took off again before they could attack. After further fruitless attempts to land at Damascus and Baghdad, it bumped down in the desert beside the blocked runway in Aden, where Mahmoud callously shot the captain, Jürgen Schumann, whom he had only two hours previously embraced in gratitude for landing the aircraft safely.

During the night the aircraft took off again under the co-pilot and, after further abortive circuits, landed at Mogadishu early on the morning of Monday 17th October. Captain Schumann's body was thrown out on to the runway.

Somalia was the base from which Wadi Haddad had organized the previous joint RAF/PFLP hijacking which had ended at Entebbe in 1975. President Barre, however, was now at war with Ethiopia, and needed friends. With some persuasion from the King of Saudi Arabia and President Carter, he agreed to co-operate with Chancellor Schmidt in a rescue attempt by the GSG9 team. The team itself was by then back in Germany; but its leader, Ulrich Wegener, had been waiting in Dubai, with two members of Britain's SAS regiment who had joined him.[1] They flew at once to Mogadishu and made plans for the assault, while the team itself was flying post-haste from Germany.

The hijackers had given Schmidt a final deadline of 3 p.m. on Monday. At 2 p.m. they prepared to blow up the aircraft with plastic explosive, sprinkling the passengers with kerosene and spirits from the bar. Negotiations from the control tower were handled with great skill by the psychiatrist, Dr Salewski, who kept the hijackers talking. In a further ploy for time, a false message was sent that the German government had given in and had put the release of the prisoners in motion. The deadline was postponed until 2.30 a.m. The GSG9 team landed just after dark, at 7.30 p.m., and put in their assault at 2 a.m. The technique, as with the Dutch at Glimmen and Assen, was to stun everyone with noise; and the hijackers, believing themselves to be on the point of victory, were taken completely by surprise. Though Mahmoud managed to throw two grenades, none of the hostages or the GSG9 troopers received more than slight injuries. Three of the four hijackers (including Mahmoud) were killed, and the fourth, a girl, severely wounded.

When Ennslin and Baader heard the news on the radio in Stammheim Prison they committed suicide, along with another of the original gang, Jan-Carl Raspe. A fourth, Irmgard Moller,

1. The growing co-operation between the world's anti-terrorist teams is encouraging. They regularly join each other for training, and Wegener himself went with the Israeli commandos to Entebbe. GSG9 men went to Glimmen in 1977 to offer help in the train hijack rescue, and were able to provide the Dutch marines with some very useful equipment and ideas. The SAS contributed local knowledge of the Gulf, as well as helping in the Mogadishu attack itself with their stun grenades.

tried to do so but failed. They made unconvincing attempts (assisted by their lawyers) to make it appear that they had been murdered by the prison staff, in the hope of gleaning at least some dividend from the disastrous operation. Three weeks later Ingrid Schubert, another of the original gang arrested in October 1970, also killed herself, bringing the total of RAF prison suicides (with Meins and Meinhof) to six.

On 19th October the body of Hanns-Martin Schleyer was found in the boot of an abandoned car in Mulhouse, in Eastern France. This was an inevitable consequence of the kidnappers' realization that Schmidt was not going to give way, either over the kidnapping or the hijacking. Schleyer's family had earlier asked to be allowed to negotiate directly with the kidnappers. Nothing came of this and it is in any case unlikely that it could have had even the effect of extending the time, since the family manifestly had no power to release Ennslin, Baader and the other convicted terrorists. Had they been released, they would almost certainly have killed more people. Hanns-Martin Schleyer and the pilot, Jürgen Schumann, had to die to save those other lives and it is clear from Schleyer's letter that he had courageously accepted this.

The final result was both humiliating and damaging to the RAF. There was worldwide disgust at the murder of Schleyer and Schumann. The German people closed ranks behind their government, whose strength and authority was reinforced, both at home and over the world. Police powers were strengthened. In the longer term the surviving terrorists may search for comfort in the fact that the public revulsion rubbed off on radical students and graduates as a whole, alienating them still further from the mass of people in Germany, to the extent that they found it harder and harder to get jobs of any kind. This could possibly drive more of them to turn in frustration to extreme politics—though more likely with the Revolutionary Cells than with the RAF. Alternatively, however, the violence, and the contempt of the third generation of the RAF for the radicals' support, may disillusion them with extreme politics of all kinds, and lead them to join the mass of the people in rejecting them.

Chapter Sixteen

Italy

A High Level of Crime

CHAPTER ONE contained an examination of the reasons why the environment in Italy was conducive to terrorism, of the growth of political and criminal terrorism and of the problems of the police, the Carabinieri and the intelligence services in countering it. The case studies in this chapter concern only criminal kidnapping, so a brief summary of the conclusions relative to that is repeated here.

It is estimated that, in recent years, 75 per cent of the kidnappings in Europe took place in Italy and that up to 98 per cent of those were by criminal gangs for ransom; that there had been nearly 200 reported kidnappings in the three years from 1975 to 1977; and that about $100 million had been paid in ransoms in five years. Most of the victims were Italians, and ranged from industrialists, bankers and merchants to the children of farmers for whose ransom whole villages contributed.

Amongst the reasons for the high incidence of kidnapping are that the prospect of gain is high, and the risk of detection relatively low. The Italian intelligence service has been weakened for political expediency, and is not helped by the existence of three separate police forces: the Police, the Carabinieri and the Fiscal Police, each under a different ministry. The level of crime creates a vicious circle, in that many policemen are assassinated, so the pressure for corruption and connivance with criminal gangs is high.

In the hope of better co-ordination, an examining magistrate is made responsible for dealing with a kidnapping. Some magistrates, in the hope of preventing the crime from paying, and of detecting fraud and tax evasion, have attempted to freeze assets or otherwise restrict free negotiation; but this has tended to drive some victims' families to settle quickly and withhold information from the police, thereby reducing the prospect of detection and conviction of the kidnappers.

THE KIDNAPPING OF CHILDREN

Italian criminal gangs, more than any others in the world, specialize in extorting money from parents by kidnapping their children. This pattern has been growing since 1973 when Paul Getty III, the seventeen-year-old grandson of one of the richest men in the world, was kidnapped by the Calabrian Mafia in 1973. When the family refused to pay the ransom demanded, the kidnappers cut off Paul's ear and sent it to them. The boy was eventually released after five months for a ransom of $2\frac{1}{2}$ million.

On 17th October 1974, Fabrizio Mosna, ten-year-old son of a rich furniture manufacturer, was kidnapped in Trento, while walking alone to school. A car pulled up and a man opened the door to ask him the way. As he leant over to look at the man's map, he was pulled into the car. He was tied hand and foot to a stake in a derelict building, where his kidnappers left him and told him to be good. He managed to escape and was taken by a passing motorist to a hospital, which had telephoned his parents before they received the ransom demand—for $130,000—which was pushed through their letter box. This kidnapping had the hallmarks of an amateurish job, done by one of the many small gangs of criminals operating in Italy.

Not long afterwards, a girl, sixteen-year-old Angela Armellini, also escaped when a similar kind of gang tried to snatch her at the gates of her school in Rome. She screamed and fought and, though the bystanders made no attempt to help her, the kidnappers took fright and ran away.

In July 1975, Cristina Mazzotti, aged eighteen, was killed by her kidnappers after a ransom of over $1,800,000 had been paid. Some members of the gang had already been arrested and the others killed her with an overdose of drugs.

Another victim (who must remain anonymous), the seventeen-year-old daughter of the head of the Italian subsidiary of a large multinational corporation, was kidnapped at 8.45 a.m. two hundred yards from her home, when being driven with her sister by a chauffeur. Six kidnappers sandwiched the car between two others and took only the older girl, leaving her sister and the chauffeur behind. Her father at first stood firm; but then he learned that the gang was led by a notorious criminal who had murdered three people while escaping from prison. The kidnappers also threatened to take the other daughter if he refused to pay. He paid a ransom of $3 million and she was released after being held for six weeks.

In July 1977, Patrizia Vallisi, aged twenty-two, was held in Milan for fifteen days by kidnappers who demanded $10 million; but on this occasion the police traced the gang during negotiations, and rescued her unharmed before any ransom was paid. Another girl, eleven-year-old Patrizia Spallone, kidnapped on her way to school, was also successfully rescued by the police.

Many rich Italians now send their children to private schools in other countries but this does not guarantee their safety. In October 1977, Italian kidnappers seized five-year-old Graziella Ortiz Patino on her way to school near Geneva, and extorted a ransom of $2 million before she was released.

RANSOM NEGOTIATIONS IN ITALY

Two examples of negotiating for ransoms illustrate the difficulties of negotiations in Italy. The second also raises the problem of multiple payment.

Filiberto Fraccari, a forty-year-old gold dealer, was kidnapped when he was returning to his home in Verona from a bar just after midnight on Christmas Eve 1975. Three men with submachine guns held him up as he got out of his car to open his garage door. Negotiations lasted for ten days, with the family trying to persuade the police to keep out of it. The examining magistrate promised that they would. The kidnappers demanded $3 million; and thereafter negotiations were hampered by spurious calls. The family offered $200,000 and eventually settled for $600,000, which was left in two suitcases in a telephone box for collection. The settlement was possibly precipitated by the kidnappers being unnerved by the arrest of another kidnapping gang.

The second victim was a fifty-nine-year-old business man who was held for a total of eleven weeks in an apartment block. The gang was almost certainly a well-known Mafia kidnapping syndicate. About forty of them appeared to be involved, ranging from three negotiators to guards who seemed to be small fry, taking no part in the decisions.

The gang demanded $2 million. After seven weeks of negotiation, $500,000 was paid. The police monitored the drop; they later arrested two men (one of them believed to be the leader), and recovered part of the ransom. The victim, however, was not released and a further ransom was demanded. The police tapping the line recognized the voice as one of a gang who were believed to have demanded double ransoms before. The family eventually paid a further $300,000, and the victim was released—but only after agreeing to pay a further $200,000 later, on pain of another member of the family being kidnapped. The total paid was thus $1 million.

PAOLO LAZZARONI

Paolo Lazzaroni, aged forty and married with two children, was the younger of two brothers who were directors of a prosperous family biscuit manufacturing business in Milan. He was kidnapped from his car, not far from the factory, at 7 p.m. on 22nd March 1977.[1] As his wife and children were away skiing, he had told his brother that he was going to a gymnasium, and then possibly to a cinema, before going home; so there was no concern about his absence for some hours. Just after midnight, the kidnappers telephoned his father-in-law, Aurelio Manzoni, who was a lawyer, and demanded $5 million. He was warned not to inform the police, was given a password, and was told to remember the caller's voice and not to speak to anyone else.

Meanwhile, however, Paolo's wife had telephoned home at 11.30 and, finding him not there, had rung his older brother

1. For a detailed account of this kidnapping see the *New York Times Magazine*, 20th November 1977.

F

Luigi, who had informed the Carabinieri. Soon after the kidnap call, Manzoni and Luigi were summoned to the Carabinieri headquarters.

Next morning, the kidnappers called again. Manzoni demanded proof of identification, and gave them a family question which only Paolo could answer. The correct answer came back in a third call at 10 p.m.

The kidnappers realized that, whether Manzoni had informed the police or not, Paolo's absence would certainly have been reported so his father-in-law's telephone was likely to be tapped. They therefore instructed him to find both a new telephone and a new negotiator, both to be unknown to the police. The family decided that it would be best to agree to this, and chose a negotiator. They confirmed that he would be willing to act but then they faced the problem of how they could give his telephone number to the kidnappers without this being picked up by the police tap on Manzoni's telephone. By coincidence, however, the kidnappers had also asked Paolo to name an alternative negotiator, and he suggested the same man; so the kidnappers rang him direct, on the sixth day after the kidnapping. They told him that they would also continue to telephone Manzoni as a cover to keep the police from suspecting the new link.

The Carabinieri, however, were having Paolo's wife watched and she was observed on a number of occasions to go into the apartment block in which the new negotiator lived. They therefore tapped all the telephones in the block until they picked up the one being used.

The family, after two hundred years in business, was cool and hard-headed. They decided early on that they would probably have to pay but were prepared to take the risk of playing for time, both to reduce the ransom and increase the chance of catching the kidnappers—in which case they might well get the ransom back.

They had therefore, from the start, said that they were raising as much money as they could, and would let the kidnappers know when it was ready. On the seventh day, the new negotiator first named a figure: $150,000. The kidnappers angrily rang off, saying that they would call again six months later.

The family then played what proved to be a masterstroke. The firm invited the press to attend a meeting of employees at the factory—both management and labour. The workers, including their Communist Party trade union leader, condemned the kidnapping, and said that the payment of the ransom would threaten their jobs. They declared that they would organize a march to the city hall to protest against the failure of the police to capture the kidnappers.

This meeting was headline news in six newspapers next day. It was the first time that workers had publicly protested against terrorism in Italy and the kidnappers were clearly alarmed by the turn of events. They rang Manzoni (meaning it for the police) and warned him to call off this 'Communist propaganda'. They then rang the secret negotiator, sounding nervous and clearly in more of a hurry to end the business. Each side said that the other side's figures were absurd, but agreed that a compromise would be necessary. The kidnappers said that they would ring again next day. Within two days they had agreed upon $730,000, about one-seventh of the original demand.

The negotiator demanded—and received—a final proof of identification. Arrangements for the drop were, as usual, complicated. The droppers were to find an envelope pasted into the telephone directory in a callbox. They were to go there immediately (the kidnappers were presumably watching the box to ensure that the police did not read it first). These instructions told them to roll up the bag containing the money in a mattress and put it on the roof rack of the car. They were then to drive at seventy kilometres per hour on a devious 200-kilometre circuit, out of Milan and back again, and to stop when told do to so. The kidnappers deployed three cars, first using two to watch the droppers' car from front and behind, and then a third to stop it at a deserted spot and transfer the money. It was taken by a hooded man, using an agreed password, and the droppers were told to stay parked for ten minutes. This was on the fifteenth day.

Two days later, Paolo's guards put him into a car and bundled him out onto a backstreet pavement. His eyes were still bound, as they had been for sixteen days—they had told him that if he ever removed the tapes or ever saw their faces they would have to kill him.

There were two guards, both obviously small fry in the gang.

They spoke always in disguised voices. During the sixteen days, Paolo felt increasingly sympathetic towards them, and they to him. Both were hooked, without hope of escape, working for a criminal gang. When they left him, one of them threw his arms around Paolo and said: 'I wish I could work for someone like you.'

How the Carabinieri monitored the drop is uncertain. Presumably all they did was to identify the collectors, trace them to their base, and then watch them until they tried to dispose of some of the money. Four weeks later, they made thirty-four arrests.

Chapter Seventeen

Latin America

A Land Fit for Terrorists

BETWEEN Cape Horn and the Rio Grande, there are twenty states. They vary widely in size, population mixture and culture, and in economic, political and social life. Latin Americans are constantly irritated by Europeans who class them all together—and still more when they refer to Latin America as a 'violent continent'. Since their foundation early in the nineteenth century, the twenty states have had no major 'Latin-American wars', even on the scale of the Austro-Prussian or Franco-Prussian wars (or of the North American Civil War)—still less any which have led to world wars. Their internal violence has never been on a scale comparable with the slaughter of Kulaks by Stalin, or of Jews by Hitler. Which, they ask, is the 'violent continent?'

Yet there has been, in many Latin-American states, a higher level of *individual* violence than in most European countries; and the size and scale of guerrilla operations has been vastly greater. Though the methods vary, the pattern is consistent and disturbing.

Terrorist Literature

For the reasons given briefly in Chapter Three, Latin-American terrorists are recruited predominantly from students and graduates accustomed to (and sometimes reacting against) a prosperous standard of living, but resentful of the uncertainty of the opportunities which their society will offer them.

Their higher education has made them the most articulate of terrorists, and the most prolific in the production of terrorist

165

literature. The Monteneros, for example, published a compre-
hensive and well illustrated manual covering the use and main-
tenance of every kind of weapon, the making of bombs and im-
provised grenades, the art of forging documents, and military
tactics ranging from the strangling of a sentry to an attack on
battalion scale. In Argentina, attacks on this scale were not uncommon in the early 1970s—though they tended to rebound on
the guerrillas. Since 1975 such attacks have been rare, and assassinations and kidnappings involving thirty to fifty terrorists or
less have been more common.

PLAN FOR A KIDNAPPING

A remarkable document was captured in Argentina in March
1972: a detailed analysis (eight typed pages, or about 3,000
words) of the possible alternatives for kidnapping a particular
American businessman by the Ejertico Revolucionario de Pueblo
(ERP).

They noted that he left home at 9.30 a.m. and returned at about
7.30 p.m. They first considered intercepting his car in the
morning or the evening. Because of the proximity of police
stations, they also examined the possibilities of studying the
pattern of his movements on Saturday afternoon or Sunday, but
rejected them; they also rejected the idea of trying to lure him
out of the house with a telephone call; and they looked in detail
at ways of kidnapping him in his home at breakfast time or in the
evening. They then narrowed the choice down to three plans to
be worked out in detail.

Plan A was for taking him on his way home from the office.
First, a telephone call would be made to ask if he was expected
home for dinner. One comrade in the office (presumably an
infiltrated or bribed accomplice) would telephone the kidnapper's
hideout when he left. Two others, near the kidnap point, would
ring the hideout every five minutes, from different callboxes
(presumably there was a row of them) to be told when he was on
the way. Six comrades in two cars would do the kidnapping. The
victim would then be taken for transfer to a van—his chauffeur
being left 'subdued' and locked in his own car. If the police

stopped them, they were to allow themselves to be searched, while comrades from a supporting car walked up to a range of one to two metres before producing guns and killing the policemen.

Plan B was to kidnap the victim in the morning from his home. (From the detail of the plan it would appear that his family was not with him, but that he had a maid or housekeeper.) Two comrades were to enter at 8 a.m. to deliver a case of wine, purporting to be a present. After a short interval, to give time for the victim to be overpowered, a van was to draw up, appearing to be from a carpet-cleaning firm. Two men were to go in and help the others to carry out the victim, rolled up in a carpet. Inside the van he was to be transferred to a box or piece of furniture; and this, in turn, was to be transferred at another spot to a furniture van parked and partially loaded with other furniture.

Plan C was for kidnapping him in the evening. Having first checked that he was in, two comrades would knock on the door at 8.30 p.m. and tell the maid that they had come to break the news of the death of a member of the family or a partner, saying that they felt they should break it to him personally. Having overpowered him, they planned to search the house, where they hoped to find 'interesting documents'. He was then to be taken out, wearing dark glasses, to a waiting car and, as before, transferred soon afterwards to another one.

The document then examined alternative plans for hideouts: preferably a house with a garage, or a ground-floor flat facing the street, in a quiet, open area. On the opposite side of the street there must be a café or bar from which a lookout could be kept. Alternatively, they could rent a flat across the street.

Six rather complicated alternatives were considered for the method of payment, including: foreign cheques made out to several people; or letters from the victim to banks where he had accounts in the USA or Switzerland; or a draft to a third party related to the victim; or by kidnapping the victim's brother as well; or by collecting the money from his son in the USA; or by getting the victim to send a letter authorizing his brother to pay. These alternatives are interesting, in that they imply that the victim's money was tied up in such a way that no one but himself could authorize its release.

Finally, the plan envisaged that, once the ransom had been

paid, the press would be informed that the victim would 'serve a term of imprisonment' while further payments were made to various institutions for distribution to 'political prisoners' relations', or to 'the people of a slum area which has shown combativeness', etc.

If all of this went according to plan, the victim would be released by again placing him inside a piece of furniture in a van and abandoning it.

Since the document was captured before any of the plans was carried out, it is impossible to say which they would have chosen but it does indicate the degree of detailed reconnaissance and preparation which a sophisticated political terrorist movement is willing to carry out.

NEGOTIATIONS AND PAYMENT

The actual processes of kidnapping, holding the hostage, negotiating and collecting a ransom in Latin-American countries have been remarkably similar to those in Italy. This has no doubt arisen partly from the circulation of terrorist literature by the Monteneros and others, and partly from the widespread reporting of kidnapping in newspapers and journals.

There have, however, been certain differences. Kidnappings in Latin America have been carried out predominantly by political rather than criminal groups; larger numbers of kidnappers have been involved; kidnap plans have been more complicated, with blocking of access roads etc., which has led to a large deployment, with five or more fire groups and auxiliary cells totalling thirty to fifty terrorists directly involved; a large proportion of victims have been expatriates, and particularly executives of US-based firms; there is, in many countries, a great deal of collusion between terrorist groups and the police, particularly at low levels, and in some countries this collusion amounts to a positive alliance between the police and selected terrorist groups against the others; and ransoms have been very much higher than in Italy.

The largest ransom of all was paid for two Argentinian brothers, Juan and Jorge Born, sons of the chairman and founder of Bunge Born, the country's largest private firm. The kidnap occurred on 16th September 1974, and ended with the payment of a ransom of $60 million to the Monteneros in June 1975.

One of the most remarkable features was that a few days before the brothers were released, a leading member of the Monteneros, Mario Eduardo Firmenich, gave a one-hour press conference in a Buenos Aires suburb, describing how the kidnap was done, announcing the terms of the settlement and calling for the resignnation of President Isabel Peron (though for very different reasons from those of the army, who ousted her in a coup in March 1976).

The Born brothers used to travel to work from their home twenty-four kilometres from Buenos Aires, with their general manager sitting in front with the chauffeur, followed by an escort car containing two bodyguards. They were often initially accompanied by a third car, which dropped off the Born family children at school. This, though it gave greater security to the children, meant that they used to leave regularly at the same time.

The Monteneros used nineteen terrorists for the kidnapping itself, with another twenty or thirty involved in guarding the hostages and auxiliary duties. The kidnap group worked in five teams; they picked a wide boulevard with narrow parallel service roads either side. On the signal that the car was approaching, they closed the boulevard under pretence of lopping the trees, and established a portable traffic light to divert traffic through the service road. Two trucks were used to collide with the Borns' car and the bodyguards' car. Terrorists dressed as policemen ran on to the scene, 'arrested' the bodyguards and, after beating them up, handcuffed them under their own car. They shot the general manager and the chauffeur dead, and took away the Born brothers.

As has already been described in two other cases (see pages 58 and 104), kidnappings in Latin America do frequently take place in busy streets in broad daylight, and shooting is commonplace. The bystanders, not surprisingly, do not intervene, and say nothing.

The process of negotiation and the dropping of ransom money is usually much on the same lines as described for Italy in Chapter Sixteen, except that in most Latin-American countries there is much greater suspicion of police corruption.

Negotiations, as in the case of the Born brothers, are often prolonged. In another case, where an executive of an American firm was kidnapped, the kidnappers' first demand was for $5 million—in US dollars. The negotiator (a local lawyer) indicated a readiness to discuss the ransom, but insisted that payment must be in local currency, and made his first specific offer in pesos, equivalent to $20,000. (All amounts will be given in dollars for simplicity.) After five weeks he raised it to $50,000, after twelve weeks to $100,000 and after nineteen weeks to $150,000. It was only then that the kidnappers lowered their demand for the first time—to $3 million. The negotiator then stood firm until the kidnappers reduced to $1 million, when he raised the offer to $214,000. The final settlement, after thirty weeks, was just over $400,000—in pesos—that is, one-twelfth of the original demand.

Throughout these long negotiations, contact was maintained with the police, who were clearly tapping the telephones. The negotiator showed patience and skill, and gained from not being either emotionally involved with the family or financially involved with the firm. He quickly appreciated that the kidnappers were professionals, and judged (rightly, as it proved) that they would not destroy their asset, the hostage. He regularly demanded proof that the hostage was alive, and the kidnappers accepted this. A degree of mutual trust was gradually established, because the kidnappers were confident that they were going to receive a ransom in the end. The police were given all the letters and tapes, and thirty weeks of negotiation should have enabled them to gather evidence for a rescue or an arrest. Even though this was not achieved, however, the ransom was reduced to a fraction of the sum for which the kidnappers held out for four months before beginning to reduce their demand.

IV. A GLANCE AT THE FUTURE

Chapter Eighteen

Prospects for Terrorism

MORE POWER TO THE TERRORISTS

A LOOK into the crystal ball suggests that terrorism will increase; and also that kidnapping will increase, but more for publicity and for money (whether for political party funds or criminal gain) than for political blackmail. This is because other types of terrorism will be progressively more effective than kidnapping for exerting political blackmail.

Terrorism will continue to plague the world because of its proven publicity dividends; because growing affluence and higher education will produce a larger number of frustrated young people whose opportunities do not match their expectations, and for whom the challenges in their lives give too little outlet for their otherwise normal aggressive instincts; because familiarity with terrorism breeds resignation to it; because of its widening international links; because of its attractiveness to national governments as a means of making proxy war; because of the growing vulnerability of industrial societies to both blackmail and damage; and because of the technological development of new weapons and other devices, and their availability to the terrorists.[1]

At the top of the scale, there is no doubt that a credible nuclear threat is within the grasp of clandestine terrorist groups. This threat might take the form either of the detonation of a nuclear device (probably consigned as a crate of machinery to some un-

1. Paul Wilkinson's *Terrorism and the Liberal State* (Macmillan, London, 1977) pages 188–206 provides a clear and concise analysis of the potential of terrorism in the light of both political and technological developments. So also does Brian Jenkins' *High-Technology Terrorism and Surrogate War: The Impact of New Technology on Low-Level Violence* (Rand Corporation, Santa Monica, 1975).

disclosed warehouse, to be fired by radio control), or of the discharge of massive lethal radiation or pollution from nuclear material. Chemical or biological weapons are equally feasible. There are, however, two major restraints: first, the carrying out of the threat would obviously be counterproductive to the terrorists (they even try to avoid killing twenty people in a bomb attack for this same reason) and, in consequence, governments would be relatively likely to call the bluff; and second, the complexity of such an operation would greatly increase the chances of detection without, in fact, wielding any more coercive power than a pistol at the head of a single hostage—perhaps less, because of the credibility factor.

Much more useful to the terrorist is the development of the power of hand-held weapons. After relatively little change for the previous sixty years (since the arrival of the hand-held machine gun) there has been a sudden burgeoning in the last decade, in miniaturization, accuracy and destructive power. There is now a pistol (the M.A.C.11) which can fire 1,200 rounds per minute, and a sub-machine gun less than fifteen inches long; both are almost completely silent. Night-vision sights are readily available. There is a disposable, silent mortar which can destroy light structures, and weighs only twenty-two pounds, including seven rounds of ammunition. There is the German 'Armbrust 300' anti-tank weapon (it can also, of course, penetrate masonry), which has no backblast, and can therefore be fired from inside a room. And there are now numerous anti-tank or anti-aircraft hand-held weapons which can deliver a guided missile with a very nearly 100 per cent chance of a hit, guided by heat-seeking homing devices, by radar or radio control, by laser beam or by wire guidance. Some of these weapons weigh thirty pounds or less, have a range of several thousand metres, and could therefore feasibly be used to penetrate either an armoured VIP car (softer than a tank) or a building, with virtual certainty of hitting it, by terrorists on foot or in a car several kilometres away.

Some of these weapons are already in the hands of terrorists. A group of Palestinians, arrested near Rome airport in 1973, were armed with Russian SAM7 surface-to-air missiles, and apparently intended to shoot down an airliner shortly after take-off. These weapons were probably supplied by Libya. In future, as new weapons become available, older models will be sold off, or given away by sympathetic governments or by unscrupulous arms dealers. The American 'Redeye' (the equivalent of the Russian SAM7) has already been superseded by the 'Stinger', and no system of end-user certificates can wholly control the disposal of obsolete models.

The development of surveillance equipment, though it will probably help the police more than the terrorist, will nevertheless widen the terrorist's options. Miniature cameras, bugging and tracking devices can make it easier for the terrorist to build up his intelligence, and to prepare and carry out his attack.

There are also now other fields of attack open to the terrorist, without the use of physical violence, but with great potential for coercion. These include interference (or the threat to use a credible power of interference) with computer systems, data banks and communication and control systems. By infiltration, by intimidation or corruption of staff, or by acquiring secret electronic information, the terrorist could acquire enormous power to blackmail either governments or commercial firms.

There is another disturbing prospect in view. The trend since 1945 has been for the number of small nations to increase, first owing to decolonization, and more recently by the secession of ethnic minorities. In 1945 there were about sixty nations in the world; by 1960, there were ninety and there are now over 150. Bangladesh broke loose in 1971. Cyprus split in 1974—perhaps permanently. There may soon be a Palestinian state. Ethiopia was in 1978 fighting to keep in secessionist Somalis and Eritreans. Whether or not such secessions are just, a larger number of small nations will increase the likelihood of some of them exploiting international terrorism to make 'surrogate war'—and the more choices the terrorists will have for seeking support for their 'internal wars', and for obtaining supplies of only slightly obsolete, but still very effective, modern weapons and equipment.

MORE KIDNAPPING?

With so much new power to kill people or destroy buildings at long range, or to use electronic and other powers of coercion, why should terrorists need to kidnap? The answer is money. The holding of a hostage in a secret hideout is likely to remain the most cost-effective method of extorting a ransom. And technological developments will help the kidnapper. Surveillance devices will help him to plan, prepare and carry out his operation. Miniaturized hand-held weapons, with greater accuracy and power of penetration, will enable him to be more selective in killing drivers and bodyguards without hitting his intended victim, and will give him more firepower with which to exploit his advantage of surprise and fight off police and army reaction forces.

The further development of the media will also encourage the kidnapper. As each year goes by, instant news reaches more people, and in more dramatic form. Over the past 100 years the growth has been exponential, and colour television now brings blood into the living room. The most significant current growth is in the field of selective retrospective viewing. Anyone who is wondering what is the latest development in a spectacular kidnapping will one day be able to flick a switch to call for the most recent news bulletin to keep his curiosity alive. If he learns that he has missed a dramatic current affairs broadcast, the television coverage will be there for instant recall—blood and all—on the screen. A sophisticated terrorist will know well how to exploit this development to maintain the tension and near-hysteria which gives him his power.

MORE POWER TO THE PEOPLE

But all these developments, in weapons, in surveillance, in communications and in the media, also give more power to society—to the people and to the police—to counter the terrorist. Given the political will to use this power, the overall advantage should lie with the police, and especially by increasing their prospects of detection, arrest and conviction.

Hand-held weapons which penetrate armour and masonry, or which home on to their target, will give more benefit to terrorists than to bodyguards or policemen. Modern personal weapons, such as rapid-fire pistols, miniaturized sub-machine guns and night-vision equipment will be equally available to both sides; but the policeman or bodyguard has far better opportunities for training than the clandestine terrorist. When it comes to the close-quarters battle, the terrorist may have the advantage of surprise; so the policeman or bodyguard must rely on training, which should give him superior skill in combat and a quicker response, to counter this advantage.

There is continuous development in equipment available to provide secure perimeters, premises and vehicles, and to provide for foolproof identification and searching of staff and visitors. Law-enforcement agents also have the power to deploy surveillance equipment of all kinds more widely and more easily than the terrorist. On the other hand, the terrorist knows that he needs to bug only one or two places, while the police may have to cover a wider front—the historic advantage of the attacker over the defender—so the police will need to exploit their wider access to different devices to counter this advantage.

There is now no technological barrier to locating the originator of any telephone call within seconds. The forbearance from installing this power into the telephone system lies in a wholly legitimate fear that it could be abused. There can, however, be effective safeguards, both technical and procedural, against such abuse. One possible safeguard is that tapping or location might be put into operation only at the (instant) choice of the recipient of the call; another that the tapping or location could itself be automatically recorded and retrospectively monitored by an independent review organization appointed by the judiciary. Some risk of abuse would remain, and the installation of the system would be expensive; but where the terrorist threat to life and liberty reaches epidemic proportions, as it has in Italy and in some Latin-American countries, this might be justified.

Other problems would also arise from the widening of telephone location and surveillance: it would drive kidnappers to make more use of other less traceable means of communication, such as letters and newspaper advertisements; it would impede the process of negotiation; and, both for that reason and because they feared that the police might react indiscreetly, the families of hostages might be further driven to try to negotiate behind their backs.

Another field of development which should benefit the victim and the public is that of smaller and more powerful tracking devices. There are already miniature transmitters which can be fitted into, for example, the heel of a shoe, or concealed about the body, or even in the filling of a tooth. Their range at present is short, but will increase. Their associated tracking systems are expensive and, thus far, bulky; but miniaturization is progressing, and their application could become increasingly cost-effective in high-risk areas. The victim, his vehicle, the terrorists' vehicle or even the terrorist himself may be more easily tracked.

A further field for development lies in finding better means of tracing the money paid for ransom. The means must be quick and easy to apply and hard to detect. We may be in sight of the day when magnetic data can be universally incorporated in every banknote, and this might pay for itself in combating the growing trends in ordinary crime. This again could drive terrorists and other criminals to turn increasingly to other kinds of currency, such as precious stones; or to other methods of payment, such as credits in foreign accounts in the names of undetected accomplices; but these too can be made more vulnerable to surveillance.

We have probably already reached the stage where the problem lies not so much in the power available from technological developments, as in the reconciliation of unrestrained use of that power with the liberty of the individual. That dilemma will grow as technology develops further; and the reconciliation will vary, as now, both with the country and with the terrorist threat.

To counter the growth of crime, and especially of criminal and political violence, police forces already require increasing support and co-operation from the public, from industry and from the security agents whom they engage to protect them. The ratio between the number of crimes and the number of policemen, in all countries, is increasing, so this trend must continue. It is already clear that industry has become the main target, both for criminal extortion and for sabotage for political ends, including publicity; and also for fraud, including computer fraud, on a massive scale. All of these can be used for criminal or political blackmail and extortion. Firms and members of the public will have to do more to take care of themselves, to avoid presenting targets, and to provide positive assistance to the police, both by relieving them of most of the task of protection against petty pilferage and theft, and by giving information.

Closer and better organized co-operation will also be needed between members of the community, between firms and between security agencies, both nationally and internationally. This can be furthered both by informal co-operation and, more formally, through industrial and professional associations. Such associations—and commercial organizations of any kind—are less hampered by political considerations in international co-operation than governments and police forces, so security co-operation on a straightforward commercial basis may be particularly fruitful. This is already practised by multinational corporations, especially in banking and the oil industry. The EEC also provides a natural association in which companies, including security companies, can co-operate in security matters, either bilaterally or as groups.

Bilateral co-operation between certain governments, intelligence agencies and police forces is excellent,[2] but the story of United Nations and other attempts at general international co-operation against terrorism, including hijacking and kidnapping, is one of continual frustration. Within the EEC, one or two member countries have been particularly reluctant to commit themselves to international action which could forfeit their freedom to pursue their own national options. Of the nineteen states of the Council of Europe, Malta and the Republic of Ireland declined to sign the European Convention for the Suppression of Terrorism in 1977. In the United Nations the Afro-Asian bloc, led by the Arab states, have consistently given the rights of 'liberation movements' priority over co-operation against terrorism in the world as a whole.

Sadly, it must be assumed that a majority of governments will continue to put national before international interests. This, therefore, underlines the importance of bilateral and multilateral co-operation between police forces on the working level, between commercial firms, and within international professional associations. This is as important as the advancement of co-operation by

2. A good example of this is the co-operation between anti-terrorist forces such as the German GSG9 and the British SAS (see page 156).

firms and peoples with their own national police forces, in their own and their collective protection against terrorism.

LIBERTY AND THE LAW

The more the public are harrassed by terrorism, the more they will demand a tightening of the laws against it; but protective laws illiberally applied may not only be repressive, but may also increase the normally tiny number of people willing to support terrorism—so tiny that a tiny increase could double or treble it, and greatly benefit the terrorists. On the other hand, the greatest deprivation of liberty is the deprivation of life; and, next only to that, the holding of a hostage not only suffering physically, but also under constant minute-by-minute uncertainty as to whether he will live or die. This is far worse than prison.

The balance of these liberties is a delicate one, and the trends are complex. Terrorist cruelty, especially against children, makes the majority ready to sacrifice their own liberties to combat it; on the other hand, if terrorism so abounds that it ceases to be headline news, then people may chafe at the restrictions needed to combat it, just as they chafe at some of the laws designed to restrict the far greater loss of life from ordinary crime, or from bad driving on the roads.

Part of the solution lies in the government and the media ensuring that people never become resigned to terrorism, or lose their revulsion against terrorists. This requires a balance in presentation of the news, which is most healthy if it can be achieved voluntarily by the editors (press and broadcasting) submitting themselves to control by their own established review body. This can be encouraged by making sure that the revulsion against terrorism taints the image of anyone in the media who supports it or fails to co-operate in defeating it.

While the prospect of conviction of the terrorist is a more powerful deterrent than the prospect of punishment—even capital punishment—there is scope for review of the penalties for kidnapping. Its victims are almost always innocent people and, as hostages, are subjected to the most horrible form of cruelty and tyranny; so it is arguable that kidnappers should be more severely punished. Whether the death penalty is productive or counter-productive varies with the country and the climate of opinion, but there is certainly a case for longer and more stringent confinement for kidnappers than for other kinds of criminal, since they have inflicted a far more cruel kind of confinement on their victims.

History has shown that terrorism can be and has been eliminated by a ruthless response to it, for the power does ultimately lie with the government and its security forces. Piracy, which seemed insoluble, was largely wiped out in the eighteenth century; and terrorism, which seemed incurable in Brazil in 1970 and in Uruguay in 1971, was virtually expunged from both by 1972—but at a price which few Western societies would wish to pay.

Whether or not kidnapping and other forms of terrorism can be contained will depend on a number of things: on the extent to which governments are willing to co-operate internationally; on the strength of their political will, both internationally and internally; on how far technological development can be harnessed to the advantage of the people and the police rather than of the terrorists; on the wise use of the law and of administrative philosophy to mobilize the people against it and to deter both criminals and political extremists from attempting it; on the acceptance by governments and law-enforcement agencies that the mass media are here to stay and to grow, and that they must develop more skill and finesse in harnessing the power of these media on their side; on the spread of public understanding of terrorism and of how it can be countered; and on the development of professionalism in the response to what has become a highly professional type of crime.

Bibliography

THESE books are selected to provide further reading about the kind of people who become terrorists, and on the organization and method of operation of a number of terrorist groups; also about practical methods used to counter them in various countries. One book (Sir Geoffrey Jackson's *People's Prison*) can be regarded as 'required reading' for anyone who wants to understand what it is like to be kidnapped. Books by specialists devoted solely to the psychological and behavioural motivations of terrorism are not included; they often confuse rather than assist the lay reader, who will probably learn more easily from the treatment of these aspects in books such as those by Arendt, Becker, Carr, Halperin, Jackson, Laqueur, Mehnert, Priestland and Wilkinson.

The latest edition of the *Annual of Power and Conflict* will provide the most convenient summary of terrorist movements worldwide. And the *Conflict Studies*, grouped at the end of the list, provide concise (10,000-word) studies of regions and countries where terrorism is most likely; new ones are published monthly and some of those listed are becoming out of date, but remain useful to the busy reader until they are superseded by others. The list given is a selection; a full list of those available is given on the inside cover of each one as at the date of issue.

The *Securitech* Catalogue, listed at the end of the selection of books, gives a useful guide to most of the security equipment on the market.

BOOKS

Annual of Power and Conflict (Institute for the Study of Conflict, London, usually published in September)

ARENDT, Hannah, *Crisis of the Republic* (Pelican, Harmondsworth, 1973)

BECKER, Jillian, *Hitler's Children* (Panther, London, 1978)

BOWYER BELL, J., *Transnational Terror* (AEI-Hoover Policy Studies, Washington DC, 1975)

CARR, Gordon, *The Angry Brigade* (Gollancz, London, 1975)

CLUTTERBUCK, Richard, *Guerrillas and Terrorists* (Faber and Faber, London, 1977)

CLUTTERBUCK, Richard, *Living with Terrorism* (Faber and Faber, London, 1975)

COHEN, S. and TAYLOR, L., *Psychological Survival: The Experience of Long-Term Imprisonment* (Pelican, Harmondsworth, 1972)

CONGRESSIONAL COMMITTEE STAFF STUDY, *Political Kidnappings 1968–1973* (Washington, 1973)

DOBSON, C. and PAYNE, R., *The Carlos Complex* (Hodder and Stoughton, Coronet, London, 1978)

GELLNER, John, *Bayonets in the Streets* (Collier-Macmillan, Canada, 1974)

GIBSON, Brian, *The Birmingham Bombs* (Barry Rose, London, 1976)

VAN DEN HAAG, Ernest, *Political Violence and Civil Disobedience* (Harper and Row, New York, 1972)

HABERMAS, Jürgen, *Toward a Rational Society* (Heinemann, London, 1971)

HALPERIN, Ernst, *Terrorism in Latin America* (Washington papers No. 33, Sage Publications, Washington DC, 1976)

JACKSON, Geoffrey, *People's Prison* (Faber and Faber, London, 1973)

JENKINS, Brian, *High-Technology Terrorism and Surrogate War: The Impact of New Technology on Low-Level Violence* (Rand Corporation, Santa Monica, 1975)

JENKINS, Brian, *Hostage Survival: Some Preliminary Observations* (Rand Corporation, Santa Monica, 1976)

JENKINS, B. and JOHNSON, J., *International Terrorism: A Chronology, 1968–1974* (Rand Corporation, Santa Monica, 1975)

JENKINS, Brian, *International Terrorism: A New Kind of Warfare* (Rand Corporation, Santa Monica, 1974)

JENKINS, Brian, *Should Corporations be Prevented from Paying Ransom?* (Rand Corporation, Santa Monica, 1974)

JENKINS, Brian, *Will Terrorists Go Nuclear?* (Rand Corporation, Santa Monica, 1975)

KOCH, P. and HERMANN, K., *Assault at Mogadishu* (Corgi, London, 1977)

LAQUEUR, Walter, *Terrorism* (Weidenfeld and Nicolson, London, 1977)

MEHNERT, Klaus, *Twilight of the Young* (Secker and Warburg, London, 1978)

OFER, Yehuda, *Operation Thunder: The Entebbe Raid* (Penguin, London, 1976)

PARRY, Albert, *Terrorism from Robespierre to Arafat* (Vanguard, New York, 1976)
PRIESTLAND, Gerald, *The Future of Violence* (Hamish Hamilton, London, 1974)
WILKINSON, Paul, *Terrorism and the Liberal State* (Macmillan, London, 1977)

CATALOGUE

Securitech: The International Guide to Security Equipment (published annually by UNISAF Publications Ltd., 32–6 Dudley Road, Tunbridge Wells, Kent TN1 1LH, England.

CONFLICT STUDIES

All published by the Institute for the Study of Conflict, 12 Golden Square, London W1.
A selection listed in order of publication:

February 1972, No. 20   By a Canadian correspondent, *Quebec: The Challenge from Within*

May 1972, No. 23   JOHNSON, Kenneth F., *Guatemala: From Terrorism to Terror*

December 1972, No. 29   POPOV, Milorad I., *The American Extreme Left: A Decade of Conflict*

February 1973, No. 33   HORCHEM, Hans Josef, *West Germany: 'The Long March through the Institutions'*

June 1974, No. 45   LECLERC, Hervé, *Marxism and the Church of Rome*

June 1974, No. 46   HORCHEM, Hans Josef, *West Germany's Red Army Anarchists*

July 1974, No. 47   EVANS, Robert Devrel, *Brazil: The Road back from Terrorism*

August 1974, No. 48   COLLICK, M. and STORRY, R., *The New Tensions in Japan*

March 1975, No. 55   BONNEMAISON, Antoine, *Social Conflict in France*

May 1975, No. 58   HÄGGMAN, Bertil, *Sweden's Maoist 'Subversives': A Case Study*

May 1975   ISC Special Report, *New Dimensions of Security in Europe*

October 1975, No. 63	JOHNSON, Kenneth F., *Guerrilla Politics in Argentina*
November 1975, No. 65	HORCHEM, Hans Josef, *Right-Wing Extremism in West Germany*
January 1976, No. 67	WILKINSON, Paul, *Terrorism versus Liberal Democracy: The Problems of Response*
February 1976, No. 68	BOWDEN, Tom, *Men in the Middle: The UK Police*
April 1976, No. 70	KLIEMAN, Aaron S., *Emergency Politics: The Growth of Crisis Government*
September 1976, No. 75	GREGORY, Frank, *Protest and Violence: The Police Response*
December 1976, No. 78	BOWDEN, T. and GOODMAN, D. S. G., *China: The Politics of Public Security*
January 1977	ISC Special Report, *The Survival of the 'Capitalist System'*
February 1977, No. 80	WATSON, Frank M., *'The Movement': Role of the US Activists*
September 1977, No. 87	PONS, Vittorio, *The Long-Term Strategy of Italy's Communists*

Index

Active Service Units (ASU), *see* Irish Republican Army
Aden, 50, 52, 155
Advisers, *see* Security, advisers
Aims of terrorists, *see* Criminal groups, Kidnapping *and* Political terrorist groups
Alarm systems, *see* Security equipment
Albrecht, Susanne, 38
Algeria, 49–50, 154
America, *see* United States of America
Anglo-Irish Bank, 137
Apolloni, Angelo, 47
Arafat, Yasser, 49
Argentina, 15, 17, 20, 29, 54–5, 60, 112, 166, 168–9
Armed Proletarian Nuclei (NAP), 42–3
Armellini, Angela, 159
Army, *see* Security Forces
Arrest, *see* Kidnappers
Assassination, *see* Murder
Assen, 121, 124–5, 141, 146–7, 156
Assets, freezing of, 46, 82, 84, 158
nationalization of, 17
see also Law
Association of Latin American Students, 55
Austria, 29, 49
Authoritarian systems, strengths and weaknesses of, 30, 71–2, 75, 78–9, 81
Autonomia Operaia, 42; *see also* Red Brigades

Baader, Andreas, 33–6, 39–40, 154, 156–7
Baader-Meinhof Gang, *see* Red Army Fraction
Balcombe Street siege, 33, 122, 125–6, 135–6
Bandero Roja, 17
Barre, President, 156

Beilen train hijack, 142–4, 147
Bejerot, Dr, 124; *see also* Psychiatrists
Belgium, 15, 47, 153
Black Liberation Movement, 53
Black Muslims, 122
Blackmail, political, 19–21, 29–30, 64, 82–3, 136, 173, 175
Böhm, Lotte, 39
Bolivia, 20, 54
Bombings, 21, 33, 53, 80–1, 137
Booth, Chief Superintendent, 133
Born brothers, 17, 29, 168–70
Boudia, Mohammed, 50–1
Bovensmilde School siege, 144–5, 147
Brazil, 54, 103, 181
Breton Liberation Front (FLB), 47
Britain, 22, 30, 32–3, 79, 81, 83, 106, 112, 121–2, 131–6, 153, 155
British Security Industry Association, 100–1
Buback, Siegfried, 38, 150
Bugging, *see* Security *and* Surveillance
Bunge Born, 17, 169

Caillol, Alain, 148–9
Calabria, 39, 46, 65
Californian State Senate, 84
Canada, 15, 53–4
Carabinieri, 44–7, 158, 162–4; *see also* Police
Carlos, 36, 50–2, 141–2
Carter, President, 156
Cell structure, *see* Political terrorist groups
Ché Guevara, 20
Chile, 15, 54–5
Codewords, 105, 108
Commando Armigiro Gabaldon, 17
Communist Party, Italian (PCI), *see* Italy
Consultants, *see* Security, advisers